THE DEEP RIG

THE DEEP RIG

How Election Fraud Cost Donald J. Trump the White House, By a Man Who did not Vote for Him (or what to send friends who ask, "Why do you doubt the integrity of Election 2020?")

PATRICK BYRNE

DeepCapture

Deep Capture, LLC

Dedicated to the cyber-ninjas and
otherwise-warriors who comprised
the
"Bad News Bears," and to citizens
who remember that, "Just
government
derives its powers from the consent
of the governed," our consent being
determined in elections that
are free, fair and transparent.

CONTENTS

"Political language is designed to make lies sound truthful and murder respectable, and to give an appearance of solidity to pure wind."

- Politics & The English Language,
George Orwell (1946)

"... the participants want the secret history of the 2020 election told, even though it sounds like a paranoid fever dream–a well-funded cabal of powerful people, ranging across industries and ideologies, working together behind the scenes to influence perceptions, change rules and laws, steer media coverage and control the flow of information. They were not rigging the election; they were fortifying it. And they believe the public needs to understand the system's fragility in order to ensure that democracy in America endures."

– "The Secret History of the Shadow Campaign That Saved the 2020 Election"

(*Time*, February 4, 2021)

"Great minds discuss ideas. Average minds discuss events. Small minds discuss people."

- Eleanor Roosevelt

Introduction

I had a ringside seat to events from November 3, 2020 to January 20, 2021, and feel a duty to tell the world what happened. I will not be regurgitating the headline events everyone will have read, but will aim to explain what was going on behind the scenes, and give my best account of why things played out as they did. My only interest is honestly conveying the truth for historical purpose.

Unfortunately, between January 9 and January 21, 2021, I had Covid-19. When I recovered, out of an interest in not letting the public suffer in curiosity any longer, from January 23 to February 9, 2021 I drafted and published parts of this story in installments on DeepCapture.com, my anti-corruption website. Thus you might think of the exercise as having been an odd one, wherein I drafted this book *publicly*, that the public need not wait to begin having its curiosity addressed. I then took those installments as a starting point to write this book, but I have substantially reorganized, rewritten, and augmented that original material.

It would be natural for the reader to question my motives, to wonder if I have an ax to grind or wish to accomplish something in writing this other than what I claim (that I feel a duty to my country to give honest account of what I saw over those nine weeks, and to do so with dispatch). So I close this introduction with four statements to clarify my philosophical orientation:

1. I have always voted Libertarian for President, and have never voted for a Republican or Democrat for President. Thus voting for Donald Trump was never a consideration for me, one way or the other.
   a. I agree with ≈ 75% of Trump's policy positions. Our nation should embody "consent of the governed," yet I do not re-

member "the governed" signing up for forever-wars; or agreeing to outsource our middle class to China; or agreeing (with no evidence or discussion) to disband our borders and do away with the Westphalian nation-state system that has served the world for three and a half centuries. I remember our *elites* doing that, but not the governed. So I agree with Trump's policy direction. I fault Trump for one thing: he should have made ethnic relations more central to his presidency, and on occasion, he tickled sentiments that shouldn't be tickled (e.g., discussing how "Mexico sends us their rapists" brought up a discussion-worthy issue, but it could have been done in a more respectful way).

   b. While I was once Left-curious, and try to maintain a position of being Left-friendly, at this point I find activist Democrats to be intellectually dishonest and lacking fundamental understanding of what made our republic work and how to fix it. Moreover, I am disgusted by the Goon-ism they embraced as a political creed far before it began making appearance on the Right.

2. Having been inside this election fraud issue for months, having gotten to know some big brains in it, professors and technologists and computer scientists, the estimate I trust the most comes from one of them, an esteemed government scientist (think "rocket science" but I may be being metaphorical to some degree). For a couple decades, this scientist and colleagues from a well-known government laboratory have been making a hobby of the study of election fraud. The final estimate of this scientist is that Donald Trump probably got around 79 million votes and Joe Biden got 68 million votes. Through chicanery, Trump ended up with 74 million, Biden with 80 million. The professor's numbers convey my rough sense of the magnitude of this election steal.

3. This steal, the "Deep Rig", should have been child's play to reveal and reverse. On December 18, President Trump and I spent 4.5 hours together: I let him know that I believed his team was trying to sink a 40-foot shot from a sand trap, but if he would just listen

to Flynn and Sidney, there was a 3-foot putt he was not seeing (I've never golfed a hole in my life, but I hoped the metaphor might speak to him). In the course of that meeting there came a moment I felt something much different for Donald Trump than I had expected to feel, something that made me want to put an arm around the man and give him a long squeeze of reassurance. What was it I felt? I'm still not sure: Commiseration for a tired man? A kind of love? Or just deep sympathy, that I could see he understood he was failing on the most colossal of scales, he was *losing*, but he could not put the pieces together? Yet it was child's play to defeat. I wanted to scold him and weep for him at the same time. Yet I hadn't even voted for him.

4. How do I *feel* about Trump? The explanation starts with my family's history as a Horatio Alger dream.

   a. My folks were of Irish working-class roots from New Jersey (Bridgeport, Paterson, Wildwood, and Cape May). My Pop was Rutgers '52 (Air Force ROTC), and my folks were living poor as church-mice at the U of Michigan, my Pop studying actuarial math, when their three sons began popping into existence. I was born last, in 1962 in Ft. Wayne, Indiana. We grew up bouncing around New England as my father changed life insurance jobs nearly every year. Passed over in 1976 in Hartford for a promotion at Travelers Insurance that he thought he deserved, my Pop took a job at a broken and insolvent auto insurer in the South: a month later an odd fellow from Omaha showed up on our doorstep, met my dad, and began investing heavily in his new employer. That same day, my Pop cancelled his order for our family's first new car (a station wagon) and sunk it into stock in his new friend's firm. My dad's new employer, GEICO, went on to big things, and my dad's investment in the stock of his new Omaha friend, Warren Buffett, also worked out well for our family. Most importantly, Buffett became my tutor in life.

   b. In the following years my family grew wealthy (by the time I was 16 my parents were millionaires, and by the time I finished college they were millionaires many times over), and Buffett grew into a billionaire and then into the mythical figure he became. All along the way, the most frequent topic of conversation among Buffett, myself, and my parents, was the role of the affluent in society, their proper behavior, their duties to other citizens and to the country (unlike lots of other rich guys, both Buffett and my Pop were always intensely patriotic men).

c. In the 1980's Donald Trump burst onto the scene with a braggadocio, gaudy display of wealth, and *loudness* in manner and taste, that was the embodiment of everything I was raised to think was wrong about rich people in America. After JFK, my parents never voted anything but Republican, but my mother did not vote for Trump in 2016, voted Libertarian (!) in 2020, and by January 6, 2021 though Trump was a madman who should be dragged from the White House. My father died in 2013, but I don't know if he would have voted for Trump in 2016, or in 2020 either. So if you wish honest account of the intellectual *milieu* from which I hail, that is it.

d. As for myself, frankly, that version of Trump that emerged in the 1980's left me so cold that I never much tuned in to him again. For example, I never once saw his TV show. Only when he ran for President did I tune in again on Donald J. Trump (see my 2019 essay, "Reflections on Donald J. Trump"). Since then, and especially in recent months, my feelings about him became decidedly more complex, as will be revealed in this book.

So that is my orientation. Enjoy the tale. I didn't enjoy writing it, but I owed it to you.

Your humble servant,
Patrick M. Byrne

Chapter 1: Why I Was Involved Before 11/3 & What I Learned Because I Was

In late July, 2020 a friend from Montana, a stolid, part Native American fellow several years my junior, visited me at home in Utah to see if I could walk again. Over the first months of the pandemic one of my legs had gone paralyzed, and in early July I had surgery on my spinal cord. When my friend saw I could walk again, he told me of a group of people, some ex-federal some not, some cyber-experts and some of other expertise, who were organizing on the subject of election fraud. He was adamant I get involved to help them. My friend was a squared-away individual, and I took his advice and requests seriously.

The next day, August 1, my friend died in a plane crash. As the coincidence was troubling, I looked into it (I am a multi-engine instrument land and seaplane pilot). It does seem to me to have been the error of his instructor, who flew the plane into a Montana box canyon without enough power to climb out.

At my friend's funeral I met some of the people he had described. A sober, quiet man with a FEMA background and a deep knowledge of bio-warfare; a retired Army Colonel with a background in Military Intelligence (including psy-ops); other men and women with backgrounds in everything from law enforcement to cyber operations in military contexts and in support of law enforcement (such as, most recently, operating against human trafficking rings in the Southwest), to the study of reverse-engineering mass election fraud.

Why were they studying the subject of mass election fraud? Because there were irregularities in the Dallas 2018 election, and those events had spawned a network of cyber-enthusiasts working on election fraud. They were convinced that industrial scale election fraud was possible, and on its way. Soon, key players were dropping through and seeing me in Utah, and I, still recovering from surgery, was driving around to meet them in other cities.

I write now of, "white hat hackers". I should make clear that I am referring to people who not only follow the law, they generally operate under contract to and at the direction of law enforcement at state and federal levels. There is a certification for working in the field of cyber-forensics, a certification that means one can crack open and image hard drives, perform forensics on them, swear out affidavits, and produce work that is admissible in court. Sometimes law enforcement uses white hat hackers in offensive cyber-missions (e.g., smashing a child trafficking/porn ring). The white hat hackers of whom I write are people with such skill sets, and who operate under contract to law enforcement doing things law enforcement needs done but which may sometimes be beyond the in-house capabilities of law enforcement.

White hat hackers also answer to other terms of endearment: "cyber-ninjas", "geeks", and "dolphin-speakers" (the last one, in honor of their tendency to congregate and squeak to each other in acronyms no one else can understand: "TCP/IP on NSF mount...")

Over September and October I was introduced by these white hat hackers to security vulnerabilities of the technology used in election equipment. Obvious vulnerabilities existed, such as the existence of RS-232 ports so that any technician who can plug-in a cord can get root-level access to the machine without a password (thus compromising the machine forever). Or an IC socket in motherboards that should be soldered shut, but which are open (so that anyone who can slip a chip into that socket for a few seconds can compromise the machine forever).

Hackers target 30 voting machines at Defcon (CNET News)
33,911 views · Jul 28, 2017   253   56   SHARE   SAVE   ...

See this CNET video, "Hackers target 30 voting machines at Defcon".

We watched hackers break into voting machines
354,439 views • Aug 11, 2017   10K   500   SHARE   SAVE ...

See also CnnTech (2017), "We watched hackers break into voting machines":

They drew my attention to strange violations of good computer science practice, such as an oddly-architected database within the machines, with three different layers but without integrity among the layers. Audit logs lacking in fixed numbering systems that could reveal tampering , and that were editable by precinct administrators (making them not "audit logs" at all).

Here is a fine 4 minute video and story from the New York Times (2018):

I Hacked an Election. So Can the Russians.

By J. Alex Halderman

April 5, 2018

f ⊙ 🗸 ✉ ↗ 🔖

"I Hacked an Election. So Can the Russians"

"All cybersecurity experts who have given electronic voting machines any thought agree. These machines have got to go... the electronic voting machines Americans got to solve the problem of voting integrity ... turned out to be an awful idea. That's because people like me can hack them all too easily. I'm a computer scientist who has hacked a lot of electronic voting machines... Imagine what the Russians and North Koreans can do... Our highly computerized election infrastructure is vulnerable to sabotage and even to cyber-attacks."

So wrote the same *New York Times* where now, two years later, the possibility of an election being hacked is now *verboten* to mention.

From Bloomberg, November 2019: "Expensive, Glitchy Voting Machines Expose 2020 Hacking Risks: Paper ballots may be safer and cheaper, but local officials swoon at digital equipment."

It came to be widely acknowledged in the tech world. See this 7 minute story "Voting Machine Hacks at DefCon" from 2018:

Voting Machine Hacks at DefCon

9,878 views · Aug 12, 2018

Here is CNN in 2019: "Watch this hacker break into a voting machine: At the largest convention of hackers in the world, voting machines were turned inside out as hackers demonstrated how easy it could be to disrupt democracy."

'Online and vulnerable': Experts find nearly three dozen U.S. voting systems connected to internet

A team of election security experts used a "Google for servers" to challenge claims that voting machines do not connect to the internet and found some did.

of hacking risks for voting systems connected to the internet

JAN. 10, 2020 / 02:51

From NBC News, January 2020: "Online and vulnerable': Experts find nearly three dozen U.S. voting systems connected to internet".

From the British Left-of-Center *The Guardian*, this in March, 2020 (ten months ago as I write): "Hack the vote: terrifying film shows how vulnerable US elections are".

This was a review of the HBO documentary "Kill Chain: The Cyber War on America's Elections", which also appeared in March, 2020. *The Guardian*'s view was that the case made by the documentary was horrifying, and they piled on with some good reporting of their own. Note that making claims now such as were made 10 months by HBO (and lauded by *The Guardian*) will today get one banned from social media, and may be illegal under the Democrats' new bill to combat "domestic terrorism".

POLITICS SEPTEMBER 27, 2019

Researchers Assembled over 100 Voting Machines. Hackers Broke Into Every Single One.

A cybersecurity exercise highlights both new and unaddressed vulnerabilities riddling US election systems.

AJ VICENS
Reporter
Bio | Follow

im Weber/The Commercial AppealZuma Press

From *Mother Jones*, September 2019: "Researchers Assembled over 100 Voting Machines. Hackers Broke Into Every Single One. A cybersecurity exercise highlights both new and unaddressed vulnerabilities **riddling** US election systems" [emphasis mine].

Lastly, Fox from 2016: "Princeton Professor Hacks Dominion Voting Machine in Seven Minutes" (posted 2020).

One day I asked the white hat hackers who had been bringing me up to speed to rate for me the security of these voting systems we were researching. I told them to use 1 = "worst" and 10 = "best" to rate the systems. Their considered answer was: "2, maybe a 1".

Let me point out that a year ago, this was not considered a partisan issue. We *all* wanted elections that were fair, free, and transparent, and we all had misgivings about where we stood thanks to these new machines. In fact, as of October, 2020 (just four months ago as I write), there probably was not a single subject one could find about which such unanimity of opinion and conscience existed across the political spectrum, as our vulnerability to mass election fraud. From *Mother Jones* to CNET to *Bloomberg* to *CNN* to *New York Times* to *Fox*, our world was in rare agreement on the subject. Only four months ago, concern over the possibility enjoyed the broadest consensus of any subject I can find.

It seems worthy of mention, given that the possibility of election fraud is now being flushed down the Orwellian Memory Hole, and may become deemed an act of, "domestic terrorism".

Beyond those hacks, they began to introduce me to other "hacks" understood in a broader sense. The extraordinary privileges enjoyed by precinct administrators, for example, to drag-and-drop queues of ballots waiting for adjudication (a point confirmed by the operating handbooks). Evidence of packet traffic going to offshore locations during elections, though we did not yet understand why this happened.

They described how in several foreign elections marred by allegations of election fraud there had been windows where vote counting was shut own unexpectedly, and in those shut-down periods there had been large and controversial swings favoring one candidate. It had happened in an African nation, and in Serbia, where the use of such systems had been involved in scandals.

A technique used in that regard that was explained to me *before* the election, was the subject of a Gateway Pundit video *after* the election:

"Drop and Roll"

How They Stole
The 2020 Election

+ — 1415 rumbles   EMBED ⟋   LICENSE

Rumble — The Gateway Pundit published several reports on how the 2020 election was stolen from Donald Trump. The numbers don't lie.
The election was stolen.

Drop and Roll' - How The 2020 Election Was Stolen From Donald Trump

They told me to watch for counting being shut down during the election. It had happened in three other nations where sketchy elections had taken place. If it happened in our election, they warned me, it would be a sign that The Deep Rig was occurring. I thought it was preposterous: who ever heard of counting getting stopped in the middle of an election, in the United States of America?

So as the weeks ticked by from late summer into autumn I came to know these folks who were convinced we were on the edge of a massive election steal. They had meetings arranged with DHS in their state, and in September, DHS officials in their state took two briefings, which were propelled up the chain of command.... only to be killed from Washington. In particular, a portion of DHS called CISA ("Cybersecurity & Infrastructure Security Agency") put the kibosh on further meetings.

Election security is within CISA's mandate: one might have thought they might be interested. After all, this was not just a ragtag bunch of misfits ("pajamahadeen" as I sometimes all them): these were professionals with extensive federal backgrounds, with all kinds of experiences of and certifications in matters cyber. They had detailed information about the security of the upcoming election, and were briefing DHS officials. Then CISA shut down their briefings.

That seemed odd, as we approached our Election Day of November 3.

In my twenties something odd happened to me from which I learned much. I had cancer three times, and spent three years in hospitals and three years more in convalescence (to know more about that bacchanal in my life, see "A PMC Threshold Moment by Billy Starr"). What I did with my time for those 6-7 years was a PhD in philosophy at Stanford. One of my takeaways from that hub of analytic philosophy, and a principle that has served me on many occasion since, is this: *The power of any theory is its ability to make predictions. That is how one tells charlatans from prophets: prophets predict the future, because their theories of the world are correct.* The dolphin-speakers with whom I had become friendly over those months had made a far-out prediction about vote counting stopping...

Chapter 2: Election 2020 – November 3

On November 3 everything they had been predicting to me would happen, happened. Counting of votes stopped, precisely as I had been warned might happen.

Not only that, counting stopped not just anywhere, but in six key locations that were anchor cities for swing states, swing states that, if flipped, also flipped the election nationally. The logic of the plan leapt off the page to anyone with a passing understanding of electoral politics.

Ask your local political science professor to explain why it is the case that to steal the national election one does not need, "widespread fraud". If the professor is honest, you will hear, "Because it does not take *widespread* fraud, it only takes *deep* fraud in six cities to flip the swing states they are in, to thereby flip the electoral college, and to thereby steal the national election. Those cities are Atlanta, Philadelphia, Detroit, Milwaukee, Phoenix, and Las Vegas."

And what do you know? On November 3, election night, vote counting in precisely those six cities took unprecedented turns. As James Woods put it elegantly, "Since when do they just stop counting votes on election day in America?" Yet counting was interrupted for three hours in various ways across in each of those six cities (it is hard to remember now, but in early November it seemed strange that they stopped counting votes on election day in those cities, though it has been normalized since).

On November 4, numerous articles appeared discussing the significance of the count stoppages. For example, see "Ballot Counting Is Delayed In These Six States With Legal Battles On The Horizon: Several of these states will ultimately end up quite close, perhaps even with recounts. Will the Election Night leaders end up losers?" (*The Federalist*, November 4, 2020) That is worth noting, because it has become another truth they wish to flush down the Orwellian Memory Hole. They are trying to convince people it never happened (though everyone I know remembers it happening, and dozens of stories appeared on November 4 describing it).

LIVE UPDATES: 2020 ELECTIONS

Burst pipe delays Atlanta absentee vote counting

A delay in processing absentee votes in Fulton, Georgia's largest county, will affect how quickly statewide results can be reported.

Voters cast their ballots at The Metropolitan Library on November 3, 2020 in Atlanta, Georgia | Megan Varner/Getty Images

By JACQUELINE FELDSCHER
11/03/2020 08:14 PM EST
Updated: 11/03/2020 08:20 PM EST

In Atlanta's State Farm Arena, a "water-main break" forced the evacuation of the vote counting area of the arena: but it later turned out to be fake ("BUSTED: Evidence Proves 'Burst Water Pipe' In Georgia Was Used As Cover For Secret Vote-Counting") . In the few hours when the counting

was "closed", hundreds of thousands of votes were pushed through the system. The "water-main break" turned out to be a urinal that had overflowed ("Reported Burst Pipe in Atlanta Ballot-Count Area Was Overflowing Urinal: Investigator").

In one location, multiple cameras caught workers pulling suitcases of ballots out of hiding and feeding them into machines while counting was officially stopped and all others had been shooed from the area:

ELECTION 2020 / ELECTION COVERAGE / OPINION / POLITICS

Georgia State Farm Arena Footage Shows Poll Workers Staying Behind, Pulling Out Suitcases With Ballots

Posted Wednesday, December 2, 2020 | *By Outside Contributor* | 🚩 **159 Comments**

f Share   🐦 Tweet   ✉ Email

A woman is seen carrying a suitcase allegedly filled with ballots without poll challenger supervision on the night of Nov. 3, 2020. (NTD screenshot)

President Donald Trump's legal team on Thursday presented surveillance footage to a <u>Georgia</u> State Legislature hearing that appears to show election ballot-counting workers kicking out poll observers late at night on Election Day before pulling out suitcases allegedly filled with ballots.

A woman who identified herself as Jackie Pick, a lawyer who is assisting with their legal case, said the team received video footage from State Farm Arena's vote-tabulation center in Fulton County, Georgia. The team said that GOP poll watchers were not allowed to watch the counting process in the poll center.

But, according to Pick, an unusual occurrence took place later in the evening at around 10 p.m. ET. A woman—described as a blonde woman with braids—told workers to stop counting and told everyone to go home.

Georgia State Farm Arena Footage Shows Poll Workers Stay Behind, Pulling Out Suitcases With Ballots

Suitcases of Ballots Pulled From Under Table AFTER Poll Watchers Were Told to Leave

Some of these cities saw goons muscle observers away from counting centers on gobbledygook reasons, while others taped pizza boxes across windows to block poll observers from observing.

In the days after the election, suspicion that untoward things were occurring was ubiquitous.

"Yes, Democrats Are Trying To Steal The Election In Michigan, Wisconsin, And Pennsylvania: In the three Midwest battleground states, vote counting irregularities persist in an election that will be decided on razor-thin margins" (*The Federalist*, November 4, 2020).

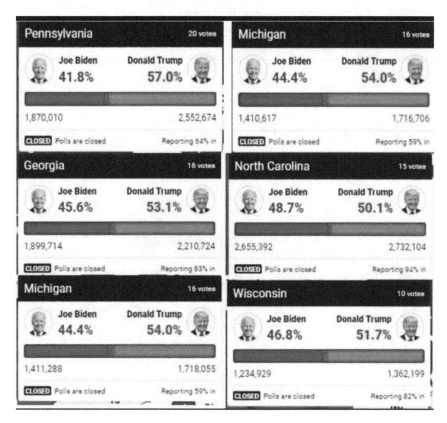

Blogs appeared with screenshots of history that could not be discounted: "WHEN THE VOTE COUNTING STOPPED ON ELECTION NIGHT, THESE WERE THE NUMBERS" **(November 9).**

Suspicion came to focus on Dominion Voting ("Dominion Machines Cover Millions of Voters, But Watch How Easy It Is To Rig One of Them" *Western Journal*, November 13, 2020). However, in my opinion that focus insufficiently appreciates the true nature of election fraud in the USA, its scope, varieties, and levels.

Within days, the cyber teams with whom I was working were coming up with data that showed what had happened in those windows where counting had been "stopped": hundreds of thousands of ballot swings, often running 99.4% and even 100% Biden.

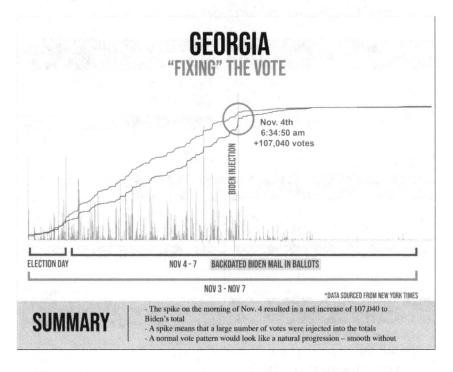

GEORGIA
"FIXING" THE VOTE

Nov. 4th
6:34:50 am
+107,040 votes

BIDEN INJECTION

ELECTION DAY NOV 4 - 7 BACKDATED BIDEN MAIL IN BALLOTS

NOV 3 - NOV 7

*DATA SOURCED FROM NEW YORK TIMES

| SUMMARY | - The spike on the morning of Nov. 4 resulted in a net increase of 107,040 to Biden's total
- A spike means that a large number of votes were injected into the totals
- A normal vote pattern would look like a natural progression – smooth without |

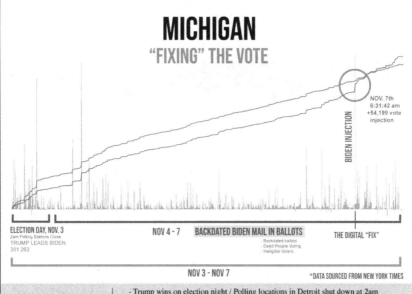

MICHIGAN
"FIXING" THE VOTE

BIDEN INJECTION

NOV. 7th
6:31:42 am
+54,199 vote
injection

ELECTION DAY, NOV. 3
2am Polling Stations Close
TRUMP LEADS BIDEN.
301,262

NOV 4 - 7   BACKDATED BIDEN MAIL IN BALLOTS

- Backdated ballots
- Dead People Voting
- Ineligible Voters

THE DIGITAL "FIX"

NOV 3 - NOV 7

*DATA SOURCED FROM NEW YORK TIMES

SUMMARY

- Trump wins on election night / Polling locations in Detroit shut down at 2am
- Ballot counters told to go home / Voting station windows covered
- Dominion Exec shows up in Detroit polling station after midnight
- Trump's election night lead disappears / Biden "INJECTION" appears

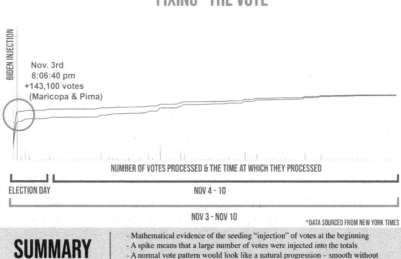

ARIZONA
"FIXING" THE VOTE

BIDEN INJECTION

Nov. 3rd
8:06:40 pm
+143,100 votes
(Maricopa & Pima)

NUMBER OF VOTES PROCESSED & THE TIME AT WHICH THEY PROCESSED

ELECTION DAY   NOV 4 - 10

NOV 3 - NOV 10

*DATA SOURCED FROM NEW YORK TIMES

SUMMARY

- Mathematical evidence of the seeding "injection" of votes at the beginning
- A spike means that a large number of votes were injected into the totals
- A normal vote pattern would look like a natural progression – smooth without extreme jumps

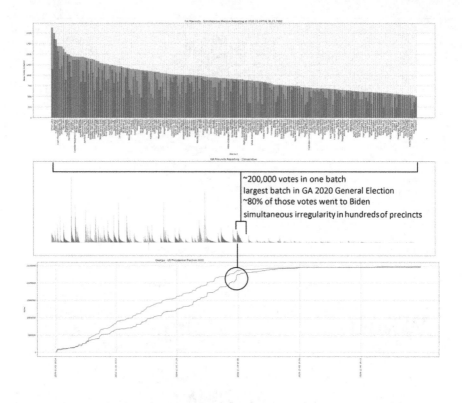

Behold a good example of a statistically impossible event our dolphin-speakers noticed as they rummaged through the data. There were occasions where a group of precincts in a state would, in lockstep, begin counting all presidential votes 17 out of 18 for Biden, 1 out of 18 for Trump. A number of precincts, simultaneously, all did that together. Then after 90 minutes, their counting would go back to normal, but another set of precincts in the state would suddenly all flip to counting 17/18 votes for Biden, 1/18 for Trump. Precisely, for 90 minutes. Then they would flip to normal, and another set of precincts would pick up the pattern. Over and over around the state. That would never happen in nature. That fact alone demonstrates that the entire election in that state should be discounted: it is 0% trustworthy.

Edward Solomon - Geometric Proof for Georgia

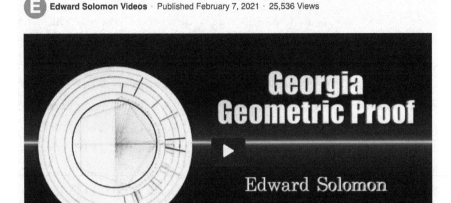

One place (but not the only place) this happened was Georgia. A researcher named Edward Solomon reported on this oddity in Georgia: Edward Solomon - Geometric Proof for Georgia

And then for Pennsylvania:

Smoking Gun: ES&S Transferring Vote Ratios between Precincts in PA. - By: Edward Solomon

PA Edward Solomon has found *disturbing* signs of statistically impossible patterns

As the dolphin-speakers and quants with whom I was working began putting such numbers together, something else happened: a self-organized digital army sprung into existence. Networks of volunteers in various states, self-organizing and diving in on various aspects of the Deep Rig: what people had experienced in polling stations, what they had been told by precinct workers, what polling observers had experienced. These networks sent delegations to find me. Soon there were witnesses to various events flying in, along with the "leaders" of networks who had found them. I was deluged with offers of assistance: volunteers from all over the country, many with backgrounds in law enforcement and military, were getting in touch through the grapevine and asking to be allowed to help in any way. It seemed that to anyone with any independence of thought, the Deep Rig was clear.

None of them wanted to be paid. At the expense of DeepCapture, people were flown to see other people and were put up in hotels to get debriefed. But no one was *compensated*.

Often I refer to the scattered organizers of these networks as, *"pajama-heddin"* (which is like being a *mujaheddin,* but you get to do it from your Mommy's basement in your pajamas). I do not mean to belittle their contribution in putting the pieces together: it was seminal. They were willing to research any question we needed answered, anywhere in the country; people willing to track down others and record experiences; precinct voters who had experienced some of the techniques of the fraud first-hand at retail level; precinct workers describing extraordinarily lax enforcement of standards; freight drivers and postal workers who had realized they were moving hundreds of thousands of fake ballots. Lawyers mobilized and researched local laws for us. People gathered sworn statements. It quickly became clear that the problem was not going to be turning up facts, it was going to be managing the tsunami of evidence that poured in. More and more Americans were stepping forward with details of things they had experienced or witnessed on Election Day. These networks began finding each other, then finding me, and I greased whatever needed to be greased until we had pulled together a team of people who could handle such a flow of information: a cyber team collecting and processing data. Affidavits were coming in by the dozens, then hundreds, and then thousands. Ultimately, I heard that grassroots organizations across America collected 50,000 signed affidavits from Americans concerning their experiences.

Some of the "irregularities" were so "problematic" they were being called out publicly by people with only modest levels of expertise. For example, in one, a web designer discussed oddities in the Edison database (provided by *The New York Times*). One of his complaints was misguided (he did not recognize the "z" at the end of the timestamp to mean "Zulu", which is to say, "UTC" or "Universal Time Coordinated", which makes his time zone analysis misguided). But in his otherwise excellent 16 minute video, he discussed other anomalies in the data that were shocking, and indicative of election fraud on an *industrial* scale. And this from someone *without* a lot of expertise.

Unfortunately, the video in question was taken down as soon as I wrote about it on DeepCapture. However, an equally interesting video is still up, one put up on November 10, that is like a time-capsule, reminding us of the election irregularities (reviewing it is a useful exercise, as the MSM will eventually try to tell you that you don't remember any of this).

Mass Election Fraud is Popping out of the Walls

Mass Election Fraud is Popping out of the Walls

One thing that drew the attention of all was the ability of bad actors to game these systems via the latitude afforded to precinct administrators. An example would be the adjudication process. This was explored with regards to Dominion machines in Georgia in two videos:

Dominion Voting Machine Flaws -- 2020 Election Coffee County, Georgia Video 1

Dominion Voting Machine Flaws -- 2020 Election Coffee County, Georgia Video 2

So what had spun up between August, 2020 and November 3 was augmented after that date by a massive flow of information from the public. That flow was filtered through debriefers and fed into a team of analysts and dedicated quants who shared insights and generated a finished product.

Due to our preparation and the assistance of so many, we quickly had a good idea how the fraud had occurred on retail, wholesale, and industrial scales in the states in question, in various permutations in each state. We knew nailing things down for the benefit of a court of law someday would require performing computer forensics, but (as I walked through above) the rough outline of the steal was child's play to see. The mountains of new statements and affidavits and data surfacing daily confirmed that larger theory.

For example, there was the Maricopa County "Sharpie Switcheroo". On election day Phoenix poll workers focused on getting voters in certain precincts to use only Sharpie magic markers, not ballpoint pens. We gathered numerous affidavits from voters who described having poll workers take pens away from them, insisting they use Sharpies, and affidavits from poll workers describing management's intense focus on Election Day (November 3): precincts were to be scrubbed of pens, and only Sharpies allowed. This "Sharpie Switcheroo" was revealed in a supervisor's email displaying weird pressure to get voters to use only Sharpies.

It all became explicable when one understands that when a machine has trouble reading a ballot (for example, as often happens when the voter uses a Sharpie), that ballot (or the machine's digital image thereof) is sent to a stack of "adjudicable" votes. Here, one *hopes* that a human (or preferably two, one from each party) reviews the ballot (or its image) and divines the will of the voter. In practice, however, it has become fodder for the "mass adjudication": that is, someone with administrator privileges could (with a mere click of a mouse) drag and drop a queue of hundreds or thousands of such votes to the candidate of choice. In other words, voters in the precincts who were steered into using Sharpies unknowingly gave proxies on their votes to their precinct administrators. And, as we saw in the previous chapter, gaining such privileges is a 100 out of a 100 proposition (per *Mother Jones* and a slew of others cited there).

Take that as a small example of the benefit of having a fusion cell where reports from the networks of people around the country was fused with insight from our technologists.

By a week after the election the cyber-sleuths and investigators with me already had things perhaps 50% sorted out. They had the strategy behind the theft: forego "widespread" election fraud and instead pick those six cities to cheat like hell, flip the states they are in, and thus flip the electoral college and the nation. More refined understandings of the strategy evolved over subsequent weeks (we found, for example, that whoever was doing the stealing in Georgia also targeted certain heavily red counties and shaved several percentage points from each). Rivers of affidavits were gushing in. People reported experiences consistent with what our team had predicted would happen under the hood of the steal, and after the fact appeared to have happened. All of this was sprinkled with statistical outliers of astronomical unlikelihood but which fit the affidavits and the technologists' insights.... and so on and so forth.

In general, as the month of November developed, people with increasing levels of expertise came forward with analyses consistent with what our own team was discovering. These were no longer people with odd things to describe from their experiences on voting day, or web designers looking at databases and seeing things that look non-kosher, but mathematicians, scientists, and econometricians elaborating on the same improbabilities bubbling up through the November 3 data that we were coming across.

Mathematicians began turning up with analyses that confirmed what we were putting together empirically, only some of which made it into the press. For example, see MIT statistician shows certainty of massive computer vote fraud in 2020 Presidential election: Dr. Shiva Ayyadurai (Dr. Shiva) provides an MIT PhD analysis of Michigan voting patterns.....

U.S. elections

Robust safeguards help ensure the integrity of election results.

LEARN MORE

Dr.SHIVA LIVE: MIT PhD Analysis of Michigan Votes Reveals Unfortunate Truth of U.S. Voting Systems.

Dr.SHIVA LIVE: MIT PhD Analysis of Michigan Votes Reveals Unfortunate Truth of U.S. Voting Systems

An excellent quant (Seth Keshel) who joined our team went on to give a rather dense analysis to the public on January 1. In truth, however, what Seth says here, he (and the team of quants he led for us) were putting together by mid-November. So for those who want to see a good quantitative explanation (with maps) which gives a sense of the kind of work we were doing in those days, watch this 20 minutes:

PureTalk - Doug Wade Interviews Seth Keshel

Doug Wade Interviews Seth Keshel

By November 12, Dr. Shiva , who holds a PhD in Math from MIT (and with whom my cyber-pals were in contact), did another thorough, quantitative analysis of Michigan Election Fraud.

Dr. SHIVA Analysis of Michigan Vote Fraud

Dr. SHIVA Analysis of Michigan Vote Fraud

Regarding Pennsylvania's irregularities, a Williams math professor laid it on the line ("Yale Trained Mathematician Flags 100,000 Pennsylvania Ballots As Likely Fraudulent"). This led to an official reaction ("Federal Elections Commission Chairman Trey Trainor says new analysis by professor Steven Miller 'adds to the conclusions that some level of voter fraud took place in this year's election'"). Professor Miller's affidavit appears over the next 5 pages: the English is quite readable (feel free to skip the parts with Greek letters).

Declaration of Professor of Mathematics, Steven J Miller, Ph.D.

1. My name is Steven J. Miller. I am over 18 years of age and am competent to testify in this action. All of the facts stated herein are true and based on my personal knowledge.

2. I received a B.S. in Mathematics and Physics from Yale University in 1996 and a Ph.D of Mathematics from Princeton University in 2002. I have published numerous papers and written several books on statistical topics, and have taught probability and statistics for the past 15 years.

3. I am currently a professor of mathematics at Williams College. I make this declaration in my personal capacity.

4. I have analyzed phone bank data provided to me regarding responses to questions relating to mail ballot requests, returns and related issues.

5. I evaluated the data provided and performed a statistical evaluation of the data and various related calculations. I provide this declaration with regard to the report presenting my findings.

6. I can show, to a reasonable degree of professional certainty, that the conclusions as stated in this report are correct.

I declare under the penalty of perjury that the foregoing is true and correct.

Steven J Miller, Ph.D. November 17, 2020

Steven J Miller, Professor of Mathematics
Williams College, Williamstown, MA 01267
sjm1@williams.edu, 617-835-3982

EXECUTIVE SUMMARY

The analysis was performed on a data set provided by Matt Braynard and his firm, Election Data Services.

- *Estimate of ballots requested in the name of a registered Republican by someone other than that person:* 40,875 to 53,909.
- *Estimate of Republican ballots that the requester returned but were not counted:* 48,522 to 44,892 (these go in the opposite order as the previous: if more of the ballots are requested by someone other than the registered voter, that means there are fewer ballots left that we estimate were incorrectly returned.).

Thus I estimate that the number of ballots that were either requested by someone other than the registered Republican or requested and returned but not counted range from 89,397 to 98,801.

Doing a more detailed analysis with confidence intervals, I estimate that almost surely (based on the data I received) that the number of ballots requested by someone other than the registered Republican is between 37,001 and 58,914, and almost surely the number of ballots requested by registered Republicans and returned but not counted is in the range from 38,910 to 56,483.

Respectfully submitted,

Steven J Miller

November 17, 2020

DETAILED ANALYSIS

I received a data set of responses to a phone survey given to people who are registered Republicans in PA. These people were contacted because there was a ballot requested in their name for the November 2020 election, but the ballot has not arrived to be counted as of November 16th, 2020; there are 165,412 such ballots.

Almost 20,000 people were called; most of the calls went to answering machines (around 14,000), had people refuse to talk (around 3000), or there was a bad number / language barrier (about 3500). There were 2684 people who answered the call on November 9th or 10th, saying either they were the person asked for or wanting to know what the call was about. These respondents were then asked several questions.

The first question was whether or not they had requested an absentee ballot; 1114 said they did, and 36 were a household member confirming the ballot request. Thus 1150 of the 2684 confirmed requesting a ballot. A sizeable number said they did not request a ballot: 531 said they did not while another 25 were a household member stating no absentee ballot was requested. This sums to 556 people confirming that no ballot was requested. Of the remaining 978 people, 343 either hung up, refused to talk, or said the person asked for is not available to talk; these 343 people were not asked subsequent questions, though there were also 91 people who said they were unsure if they had requested a ballot were asked the next question. The remaining 544 people answered that they voted in person and were not asked any additional questions; this response complicates the analysis as you cannot vote in person if you requested a ballot unless you bring the ballot to be cancelled. From the response 'voted in person at the polls' it is unclear if they requested an absentee ballot; we will thus do the analysis assuming they all requested and assuming none of them requested.

We have 1241 people moving on to Question 3 (those who answered yes, had a family member answer yes, or were unsure). Of these, 463 mailed back their ballot (though there is no record of their ballot being received; 452 said they mailed back their ballot and 11 were family members saying it was mailed) and 643 said they had not mailed back their ballot (632 said they had not, 11 had family members say it was not mailed). The remaining people were unsure, refused to speak, hung up, or were not the right person.

Our goal is to try to estimate the number of fraudulent ballots in PA from these responses, and thus correct the totals across the commonwealth. We start with the 165,412 people who were recorded as having requested a ballot but no ballot had arrived. From Question 2 there were 1150 who confirmed requesting a ballot and 556 who did not (this is ignoring the 91 who were unsure and the 544 who said they voted in the polls). Thus we have 556 out of 1706 who said the did not request a ballot but one was requested in their name, which is about 32.59%. If we multiply the 165,412 ballots requested but unreturned by 32.59%, we get about 53,909 ballots. Thus we estimate there are almost 54,000 ballots in the commonwealth that were requested by someone other than the registered Republican in whose name it was.

What if we include the 544 people who answered Question 2 by saying they voted in person at the polls? If we assume all of these people brought their ballots with them to be voided, this raises the denominator from 1706 to 2250 for a percentage of around 24.18% (down from the 32.59% before). If we extrapolate *this* number to the 165,412 ballots we now have 40,875 ballots across PA that were requested by someone other than the person in whose name they were recorded (while this is lower than the 54,000 it is still a significant fraction of the roughly 70,000 votes separating Biden and Trump.

We now turn to estimating the number of ballots requested by registered Republicans who thought they returned them but which have not arrived and been counted (as of November 16th, 2020). From the responses,

2

463 people out of 1150 (or around 40.26%) said they had requested a ballot and sent it back; however, these ballots have not been counted. We need to figure out what number to apply this percentage to. We started with 165,412 ballots and now remove the estimated 53,909 ballots that were not requested by registered Republicans in their name to get there were 111,503 ballots requested by registered Republicans in PA. Multiplying this by 40.26% yields 44,892 Republican ballots that the requesters returned but were not counted.

If instead we remove the lower estimate of 40,875 ballots (for the number of ballots requested in someone's name but not by them) and subtract that from 165,412 we get 120,520 ballots requested by registered Republicans in PA. Multiplying this by 40.26% yields 48,522 Republican ballots that the requester returned but were not counted.

EXTENSION: CONFIDENCE INTERVALS

We can do a more detailed analysis and obtain confidence intervals. If we have a large number of data points (usually more than 30 suffice; as we are in the hundreds to thousands there are no concerns) and we observe in a sample of size n of a population of size N that x have a property, we can extrapolate that to how many in the entire population have the property.

The simplest estimate is that the proportion in the sample with the property is p = x/n. so the number in the entire population is just pN = x N / n. The difficulty with that is small errors in our estimate of the proportion in the sample scale. Thus we frequently construct 95% and 99% confidence intervals.

If each person from the population of size N is independently chosen to be in the sample of size n, and each person has the same probability p of having the desired property, then the number of people in the sample with the property can be approximated by a normal distribution. We have 95% of the mass of the normal is within 1.96 standard deviations of the mean, and 99% is within 2.576 standard deviations. This leads to the following confidence intervals, where below p is the observed sample proportion having the property (p = x/n):

- 95% confidence interval for the probability: $p - 1.96 \sqrt{\frac{p(1-p)}{n}}$ to $p + 1.96 \sqrt{\frac{p(1-p)}{n}}$

- 99% confidence interval for the probability: $p - 2.576 \sqrt{\frac{p(1-p)}{n}}$ to $p + 2.576 \sqrt{\frac{p(1-p)}{n}}$

Once we have these, we can extrapolate to the entire population by multiplying by N:

- 95% confidence interval for the number with property: $p - 1.96 N \sqrt{\frac{p(1-p)}{n}}$ to $p + 1.96 N \sqrt{\frac{p(1-p)}{n}}$

- 99% confidence interval for the number with property: $p - 2.576 N \sqrt{\frac{p(1-p)}{n}}$ to $p + 2.576 N \sqrt{\frac{p(1-p)}{n}}$

We now apply this to our problem. For the first question, we had either 556 out of 1706 who said they did not request a ballot but we know one was requested in their name, or (including the 544 who said they voted in person) we have 556 out of 2250.

- 95% confidence interval for the probability: [30.46%, 34.92%] or [22.93%, 26.49%],
- 99% confidence interval for the probability: [29.76%, 35.62%] or [22.37%, 27.05%].

We can use this to estimate the number of ballots requested by someone other than the registered Republican:
- 95% confidence interval for such ballots: [50,380, 57,755] or [37927, 43823],
- 99% confidence interval for such ballots: [49,222, 58,914] or [37001, 44750].

Thus we estimate the number of ballots requested by someone other than the registered Republican in PA for the 2020 election is almost surely between 49,222 and 58,914 (if we assume the 544 who said they voted in person did not request an absentee ballot), or between 37,001 and 44,750 (if we assume the 544 who said they voted in person did request an absentee ballot). Thus almost surely the number of ballots requested by someone other than the registered Republican is between 37,001 and 58,914.

We can apply a similar analysis to the number of ballots that responders said were returned but were not received. Here we have 463 of 1150 registered Republicans saying they had requested and returned a ballot, but as of November 16th, 2020 no ballot in their name had arrived to be counted. It is easy to construct 95% and 99% confidence intervals for these probabilities (we observed 40.26%).

- 95% confidence interval for the probability: [37.43%, 43.10%],
- 99% confidence interval for the probability: [36.54%, 43.99%].

To estimate a 95% or 99% confidence interval we need to know how many ballots to remove from the 165,412. We can compute this many different ways, but in the interest of obtaining the simplest, widest range we can look at the high and low values from the above analysis of what to subtract from 165,412: 37,001 and 58,914. Thus using the 99% confidence interval values we obtain that almost surely the number of ballots requested by registered Republicans and returned but not counted is in the range from 38,910 to 56,483.

Respectfully submitted,

Steven J Miller

November 17, 2020

By the end of 2020 noted economist John Lott would come out with a paper: "A Simple Test for the Extent of Vote Fraud with Absentee Ballots in the 2020 Presidential Election: Georgia and Pennsylvania Data".

A Simple Test for the Extent of Vote Fraud with Absentee Ballots in the 2020 Presidential Election: Georgia and Pennsylvania Data

25 Pages · Posted: 29 Dec 2020 · Last revised: 11 Jan 2021

John R. Lott
Crime Prevention Research Center

Date Written: December 21, 2020

Abstract

This study provides two methods to measure vote fraud in the 2020 presidential election, though they provide varying degrees of evidence for fraud. To try isolating the impact of a county's vote-counting process and the potential fraud, I first compare voting precincts in a county with alleged fraud to adjacent similar precincts in neighboring counties with no allegations of fraud. In measuring the difference in President Trump's vote share of the absentee ballots for these adjacent precincts, we account for the difference in his vote share of the in-person voting and the difference in registered voters' demographics. I compare data for the 2016 and 2020 presidential elections. There is some weak but inconsistent evidence of vote fraud for Georgia and Pennsylvania. In Pennsylvania, the evidence is strongest for the provisional ballots. Voters were allowed to correct defects in absentee ballots using a provisional ballot on Election day – implying an additional 6,700 votes for Biden.

Second, vote fraud can increase voter turnout rate. Increased fraud can take many forms: higher rates of filling out absentee ballots for people who hadn't voted, dead people voting, ineligible people voting, or even payments to legally registered people for their votes. However, the increase might not be as large as the fraud if votes for opposing candidates are either lost, destroyed, or replaced with ballots filled out for the other candidate. The estimates here indicate that there were 70,000 to 79,000 "excess" votes in Georgia and Pennsylvania. Adding Arizona, Michigan, Nevada, and Wisconsin, the total increases to up to 289,000 excess votes.

Keywords: Vote Fraud, absentee ballots, voter turnout rate

JEL Classification: K14

Lott's findings were summarized in the popular press, "Expert: Biden win 'suspicious,' 289,000 election-changing 'excess' votes".

And so on and so forth.

I have recounted how I got involved in this; what I was warned election fraud would look like; how what occurred matched the prediction; and how the Deep Rig was reverse-engineered by a team of cyber-ninjas, augmented by a platoon of volunteers, with assistance of networks around the country, all within the month of December. In the process I provided dozens of links you can go to for further information. Therefore I will assume that any reasonable reader who has made it thus far must have at least some doubt about the integrity of the election.

This is all before considering foreign mischief in Election 2020, which is the subject to which I now turn.

Chapter 3: Was There Foreign Interference?

The occasion was a 1950's drunken Hollywood party. The leading men of the day were holding an impromptu contest of a certain immature form. Jackie Gleason famously shouted to Milton Berle: "Hey Miltie, do us all a favor and only pull out enough to win!"

I will follow that principle here, presenting only enough evidence to convince anyone open to being convinced.

On the dictum that "a picture is worth 1,000 words," I start with the question: Are any Dominion machines made in China?

Taken December, 2020
Photograph by Mark Cook

Case closed.

———————————————————————————————————

Let us turn to what the MSM and the US government were saying in the days up to the election:

- "U.S. agencies mount major effort to prevent Russian interference in the election even though Trump downplays threat" (*Washington Post*, October 21, 2020) which paints a rather breathless picture of then-ongoing foreign attempts to alter out election.
- "Iranian Advanced Persistent Threat Actor Identified Obtaining Voter Registration Data" (co-authored by CISA and the FBI, published October 30, 2020, updated November 3, 20202). As they wrote succinctly: "CISA and the FBI are aware of an Iranian advanced persistent threat (APT) actor targeting U.S. state websites—to include election websites. CISA and the FBI assess this

actor is responsible for the mass dissemination of voter intimidation emails to U.S. citizens and the dissemination of U.S. election-related disinformation in mid-October 2020. 1 (Reference FBI FLASH message ME-000138-TT, disseminated October 29, 2020). Further evaluation by CISA and the FBI has identified the targeting of U.S. state election websites was an intentional effort to influence and interfere with the 2020 U.S. presidential election." If you read through this book, you will understand the Iranian role in our Nevada elections, in particular.

So, to summarize thus far: at least *some* Dominion Machines *are* made in China, and in the 12 days before the election, the *WashPost* reported on, "US Agencies mount[ing] a major effort to prevent foreign (in this case, Russian) interference in the election". Meanwhile, CISA (part of DHS) and FBI co-authored a communique the three days before the election regarding other foreign (in this case, Iranian) "Advanced Persistent Threat" actors interfering in the election. It does not take reading far either into the CISA-FBI report, or the Washington Post article, to understand that our federal government was fighting an onslaught of foreign attempts to interfere in our elections, in the days before the election.

As the two documents just cited make clear, in the weeks and days leading up to Election Day, foreign elements were coming at us teeth-toes-and-fingernails trying to interfere in our election. On Election Day, what happened? A statement by a retired senior military officer lays things out rather clearly (there is a fair bit of "dolphin-speak" below, but if that bothers you, just skim it looking for the sections in English, and you will understand it just fine):

———————————————————————————————————

Declaration of XXXXXXXX

1. My name is XXXXXXXXXXXXXXXXXXXX, and I am a resident of XXXXXXXXXX. I hold an MBA from XXXXXX University, and a Bachelor of Science from XXXXXX University. I am retired from the US Army where I worked as an Air Cavalry Officer, a Psychological Operations Officer, and Information Operations

Officer. I specifically conducted Special Technical Operations, analyzed and applied All-Source Intelligence to operational requirements. With a specialized team of military members, I helped author the Joint Urgency of Needs Statement for the CAUI EXORD (Countering Adversary Use of the Internet) and stood up the first two special category cyber-enabled operations under a unique Secretary of Defense authority. I am currently the manager of a Cybersecurity Company based in Texas. Our emphasis is on digital forensics and incident response (DFIR) cybersecurity, analysis of publicly available information (PAI), penetration testing of networks, and problem solving through operations integration. We use state-of-the-art tools and employ a wide variety of cyber and cyberforensic analysts. My colleague and I are currently contracted to a cybersecurity and forensics firm that focuses on election systems.

2. We have examined the various Companies, Networks, Structures, Machines and related global infrastructures directly tied to the US Election.

3. This is a preliminary report on the various aspects of FOREIGN INTERFERENCE as defined by Executive Order 13848 issued on September 12, 2018.

   a. *Section 8 (f) defines the term "foreign interference," with respect to an election, to include any covert, fraudulent, deceptive, or unlawful actions or attempted actions of a foreign government, or of any person acting as an agent of or on behalf of a foreign government, undertaken with the purpose or effect of influencing, undermining confidence in, or altering the result or reported result of, the election, or undermining public confidence in election processes or institutions.*

   b. *There is clear and definitive evidence that foreign interference, as defined in the above Executive Order, occurred prior to, and during, the General Election on November 3, 2020.*

   c. *In addition, Section 1 (b)(ii) states "if any foreign interference involved activities targeting the infrastructure of, or pertaining to, a political organization, campaign, or candidate, the extent to which such activities materially affected the security or in-*

tegrity of that infrastructure, including by unauthorized access to, disclosure or threatened disclosure of, or alteration or falsification of, information or data."

d. *There is also clear and definitive evidence that foreign interference and unauthorized access to information and data, as defined in the Executive Order above, occurred prior to, and during, the General Election on November 3, 2020.*

Dominion Voting Systems and Scytl/Clarity Elections:

4. Dominion Voting Systems is owned and controlled by foreign entities. We lose control of the data when it goes to a foreign country. For example:

• The electronic information went to Germany, Barcelona, Serbia, and Canada

• Dominion Servers in Belgrade Serbia. P 82.117.198.54 (ASN Range: 82.117.192.0/19)

• Dominion Servers ftp.dominionvoting.com with IP 69.172.237.100 (ASN Range: 69.172.236.0/22) is located in Toronto, Canada

• www.scytl.com with IP 52.57.209.147 (ASN Range: 52.57.0.0/16) is (was) located in Frankfurt Germany

• support.scytl.com with IP 213.27.248.118 (ASN Range: 213.27.128.0/17) is located in Barcelona, Spain

• scytl-com.mail.protection.outlook.com with IP 104.47.10.36 (ASN Range: 104.40.0.0/13) is located in Ireland

• On election night the DE-CIX Frankfurt there was a 30% spike over the previous high rate of traffic. One stated probable cause was increased data flow to servers supporting the US Election.

Dominion Voting Systems and related companies are owned or heavily controlled and influenced by foreign agents, countries, and interests. The forensic report we prepared found that "the Dominion Voting System is intentionally and purposefully designed with inherent errors to create systemic fraud and influence election results".

5. The system intentionally generates an enormously high number of ballot errors...The intentional errors lead to bulk adjudication of bal-

lots with no oversight, no transparency, and no audit trail. This is the exact type of issue that leads to voter and/or election fraud.

6. The report found the election management system to be wrought with unacceptable vulnerabilities— including access to the internet— a key indicator to find evidence of fraud, and numerous malicious actions.

7. The numerous similarities will find that Dominion Voting Systems, Smartmatic, Electronic Systems & Software, and Hart Inter Civic, Clarity Election Night Reporting, Edison Research, Sequoia, Scytl, and similar or related entities, agents or assigns, have the same flaws and were subject to foreign interference in the 2020 election in the United States.

8. These systems bear the same crucial code "features" and defects that allowed the same outside and foreign interference in our election, in which there is the probability votes were in fact altered and manipulated contrary to the will of the voters.

   a. *Each of the companies use EML (Election Markup Language) and are susceptible to cross site scripting attacks (XSS) as described on page 7 in the Joint Cybersecurity Advisory.*

   b. *Cross-site scripting (also known as XSS) is a web security vulnerability that allows an attacker to compromise the interactions that users have with a vulnerable application. It allows an attacker to circumvent the same origin policy, which is designed to segregate different websites from each other. Cross-site scripting vulnerabilities normally allow an attacker to masquerade as a victim user, to carry out any actions that the user is able to perform, and to access any of the user's data. If the victim user has privileged access within the application, then the attacker might be able to gain full control over all of the application's functionality and data.*

   c. *Most, if not all, related sites were created using WordPress. WordPress currently has 2,675 CVE (Common Vulnerabilities and Exposures) listed on cve.mitre.org.*

d. *I performed a OpenVAS Vulnerability assessment for both Dominion and Scytl. There were multiple issues related to, out-of-date plugins and themes, which leaves sites vulnerable to attack.*

e. *With the various mergers, acquisitions, license agreements and partnerships the entire Election ecosystem in the United States is one and the same of any other Country where these systems are based, created, designed, used and so on. Namely Venezuela and their investment into Smartmatic.*

    i. *Dominion's purchase of Sequoia Voting Systems from Smartmatic has resulted in the same "Source Code" being used today.*

    ii. *During the Forensic audit we observed WinEDs and GEMS in the Dominion Voting System EMS (Election Management System). Both of those modules have been included in adverse findings from the EAC but are still in use today.*

    iii. *With the overlap between Dominion and Smartmatic, including the shared address in Barbados, the FCC Report ID: 2AGVK-VIU811 issued by the CCIS Lab in Shenzhen, China is very concerning. The Voter Identification Unit report was issued on July 23, 2020 and would give China insight on how to exploit the voting machines used in the US Election.*

9. Dominion Voting Systems is based in Toronto, Canada, and assigns its intellectual property including patents on its firmware and software and trademarks to Hong Kong and Shanghai Bank Corporation (HSBC), a bank with its foundation in China and its current headquarters in London, United Kingdom.

10. Multiple expert witnesses and cyber experts identified acts of foreign interference in the election prior to November 3, 2020 and continued in the following weeks. In fact, there is evidence of a massive cyber-attack by foreign interests on our crucial national infrastructure surrounding our election—not the least of which was the hacking of the voter registration system by Iran. (E.O. 13800 of May 11, 2017)

11. This is compounded by the magnitude of the Solar Winds exploit that has exposed the private, public and government related companies and agencies. This includes the companies and agencies directly involved with securing our elections.

12. The FBI and CISA issued a joint Cybersecurity Advisory on October 30, 2020 (Report ID: AA20-304A).

    a. This joint cybersecurity advisory was coauthored by the Cybersecurity and Infrastructure Security Agency (CISA) and the Federal Bureau of Investigation (FBI). CISA and the FBI are aware of an Iranian advanced persistent threat (APT) actor targeting U.S. state websites—to include election websites. CISA and the FBI assess this actor is responsible for the mass dissemination of voter intimidation emails to U.S. citizens and the dissemination of U.S. election-related disinformation in mid-October 2020.1 (Reference FBI FLASH message ME-000138-TT, disseminated October 29, 2020). Further evaluation by **CISA and the FBI has identified the targeting of U.S. state election websites was an intentional effort to influence and interfere with the 2020 U.S. presidential election.**

13. Dominion and Smartmatic share a physical address in Barbados despite their insistence that there is no relationship between the companies. They also have a mutual non- compete agreement detailing shared resources and code.

14. Hootan Yaghoobzadeh is the CEO and Chairman of Staple Street Capital, which is the entity that owns Dominion. Yaghoobzadeh was a close confidant to Sadaam Hussein and worked for the Saudi Bin Laden group. He previously worked at the Carlyle Group and Cerberus Capital Management.

Staple Street Partners

15. Staple Street Partners is a Private Equity firm that owns Dominion Voting Systems.

16. 9/25/19 – Dominion Voting Systems based in Toronto entered into a Security Agreement with HSBC Bank, assigning all intellectual

property and assets including Trademarks, Patents and Software (see below).

17. 10/8/20 – $400,000,000 from UBS Securities a Chinese managed subsidiary of UBS Global AG (see below).

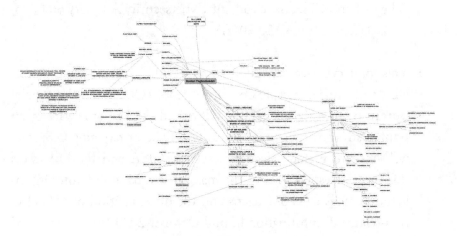

PATENT ASSIGNMENT COVER SHEET

Electronic Version v1.1
Stylesheet Version v1.2

EPAS ID: PAT5739006

SUBMISSION TYPE:	NEW ASSIGNMENT
NATURE OF CONVEYANCE:	SECURITY AGREEMENT

CONVEYING PARTY DATA

Name	Execution Date
DOMINION VOTING SYSTEMS CORPORATION	09/25/2019

RECEIVING PARTY DATA

Name:	HSBC BANK CANADA, AS COLLATERAL AGENT
Street Address:	4TH FLOOR, 70 YORK STREET
City:	TORONTO
State/Country:	CANADA
Postal Code:	M5J 1S9

PROPERTY NUMBERS Total: 18

Property Type	Number
Patent Number:	8844813
Patent Number:	8913787
Patent Number:	9202113
Patent Number:	8195505
Patent Number:	9870666
Patent Number:	9710988
Patent Number:	9870667
Patent Number:	7111782
Patent Number:	7422151
Patent Number:	D599131
Patent Number:	D521050
Patent Number:	D515619
Patent Number:	D521051
Patent Number:	D537469
Patent Number:	8714450
Patent Number:	8910865
Patent Number:	8864026
Patent Number:	8876002

CORRESPONDENCE DATA

Schedule A

Intellectual Property

U.S. Patents & Applications

Title	SERIAL #	FILED DATE	PATENT NO.	ISSUE DATE	STATUS
Electronic Correction of Voter-Marked Paper Ballot	13/476,836	5/21/2012	8,844,813	9/30/2014	Issued
Ballot Adjudication in Voting Systems Utilizing Ballot Images	13/470,091	5/11/2012	8,913,787	12/16/2014	Issued
Ballot Adjudication in Voting Systems Utilizing Ballot Images (continuation of U.S. Patent 8913787)	14/539,684	11/12/2014	9,202,113	12/1/2015	Issued
System, Method and Computer Program for Vote Tabulation with an Electronic Audit Trail	11/121,997	5/5/2005	8,195,505	6/5/2012	Issued
System, Method and Computer Program for Vote Tabulation with an Electronic Audit Trail	13/463,536	5/3/2012	9,870,666	1/16/2018	Issued
System, Method and Computer Program for Vote Tabulation with an Electronic Audit Trail	13/525,187	6/15/2012	9,710,988	7/18/2017	Issued
System, Method and Computer Program for Vote Tabulation with an Electronic Audit Trail	13/525,208	6/15/2012	9,870,667	1/16/2018	Issued
Systems and Methods for Providing Security in a Voting Machine	10/811,969	3/30/2004	7,111,782	9/26/2006	Issued
Systems and Methods for Providing Security in a Voting Machine	11/526,028	9/25/2006	7,422,151	9/9/2008	Issued
Voting Booth	29/324,281	9/10/2008	D599,131	9/1/2009	Issued
Voting Terminal and Stand	29/209,554	7/15/2004	D521,050	5/16/2006	Issued
Pair of Enclosure Doors	29/209,579	7/15/2004	D515,619	2/21/2006	Issued
Voting Terminal	29/209,556	7/15/2004	D521,051	5/16/2006	Issued
Voting Terminal and Keypad	29/254,483	2/23/2006	D537,469	2/27/2007	Issued
Systems and Methods for Transactional Ballot Processing, and Ballot Auditing	13/092,600	4/22/2011	8,714,450	5/6/2014	Issued
Ballot Level Security Features for Optical Scan Voting Machine Capable of Ballot Image Processing, Secure Ballot Printing, and Ballot Layout Authentication and Verification	13/092,599	4/22/2011	8,910,865	12/16/2014	Issued
Ballot Image Processing System and Method for Voting Machines	13/092,606	4/22/2011	8,864,026	10/21/2014	Issued
Systems for Configuring Voting Machines, Docking Device for Voting Machines, Warehouse Support and Asset Tracking of Voting Machines	13/092,604	4/22/2011	8,876,002	11/4/2014	Issued

Ownership of the above-referenced patents has been assigned to Dominion Voting Systems Corporation.

Canadian Patent Application

Title	APPLICATION #	FILED DATE	STATUS
SYSTEM, METHOD AND COMPUTER PROGRAM FOR VOTE TABULATION WITH AN ELECTRONIC AUDIT TRAIL	2466466	5/5/2004	Pending

Dominion Voting Systems is listed in the Canadian Patent Office records as the current owner of record for the above-referenced patent application, but this application is to be assigned to Dominion Voting Systems Corporation post-Closing pursuant to the Undertaking.

U.S. Registered Trademarks

Trademark	Serial #	File Date	Reg #	Reg Date	Status	Class
	85407877	Aug-25-2011	4174339	Jul-17-2012	Registered	35 37 40 41
DOMINION VOTING	85407870	Aug-25-2011	4174338	Jul-17-2012	Registered	9 35 37 40 41
DEMOCRACY SUITE	85407749	Aug-25-2011	4153203	Jun-5-2012	Registered	9
IMAGECAST	85407735	Aug-25-2011	4131899	Apr-24-2012	Registered	9
AUDITMARK	85407731	Aug-25-2011	4269144	Jan-1-2013	Registered	9
ASSURE	78440857	Jun-24-2004	3080674	Apr-11-2006	Registered	9
AVC ADVANTAGE	73755922	Sep-30-1988	1537309	May-2-1989	Registered	9
AVC EDGE	75404858	Dec-11-1997	2261646	Jul-13-1999	Registered	9
OPTECH	73689072	Oct-13-1987	1524218	Feb-14-1989	Registered	9
OPTECH INSIGHT	76624215	Dec-9-2004	3044159	Jan-17-2006	Registered	9

Ownership of the above-referenced trademarks has been assigned to Dominion Voting Systems Corporation.

The Securities and Exchange Commission has not necessarily reviewed the information in this filing and
has not determined if it is accurate and complete.
The reader should not assume that the information is accurate and complete.

UNITED STATES SECURITIES AND EXCHANGE COMMISSION
Washington, D.C. 20549
FORM D

Notice of Exempt Offering of Securities

OMB APPROVAL	
OMB Number:	3235-0076
Estimated average burden hours per response:	4.00

1. Issuer's Identity

CIK (Filer ID Number)

Previous Names   [X] None

Entity Type

0001827586

Name of Issuer

STAPLE STREET CAPITAL III, L.P.

Jurisdiction of Incorporation/Organization

DELAWARE

Year of Incorporation/Organization

[ ] Over Five Years Ago

[X] Within Last Five Years (Specify Year) 2020

[ ] Yet to Be Formed

[ ] Corporation

[X] Limited Partnership

[ ] Limited Liability Company

[ ] General Partnership

[ ] Business Trust

[ ] Other (Specify)

2. Principal Place of Business and Contact Information

Name of Issuer

STAPLE STREET CAPITAL III, L.P.

Street Address 1		Street Address 2	
1290 AVENUE OF THE AMERICAS, 10TH FLOOR			
City	State/Province/Country	ZIP/PostalCode	Phone Number of Issuer
NEW YORK	NEW YORK	10104	(212) 613-3100

3. Related Persons

Last Name	First Name	Middle Name
OWENS	STEPHEN	D.

Street Address 1	Street Address 2	
1290 AVENUE OF THE AMERICAS, 10TH FLOOR		
City	State/Province/Country	ZIP/PostalCode
NEW YORK	NEW YORK	10104

Relationship: [X] Executive Officer [ ] Director [X] Promoter

Clarification of Response (if Necessary):

Last Name	First Name	Middle Name
YAGHOOBZADEH	HOOTAN	
Street Address 1	Street Address 2	
1290 AVENUE OF THE AMERICAS, 10TH FLOOR		
City	State/Province/Country	ZIP/PostalCode
NEW YORK	NEW YORK	10104

Relationship: [X] Executive Officer [ ] Director [X] Promoter

Clarification of Response (if Necessary):

4. Industry Group

[ ] Agriculture

Banking & Financial Services

  [ ] Commercial Banking

  [ ] Insurance

  [ ] Investing

  [ ] Investment Banking

  [X] Pooled Investment Fund

    [ ] Hedge Fund

    [X] Private Equity Fund

    [ ] Venture Capital Fund

    [ ] Other Investment Fund

    Is the issuer registered as an investment company under the Investment Company Act of 1940?

    [ ] Yes   [X] No

  [ ] Other Banking & Financial Services

[ ] Business Services

Energy

  [ ] Coal Mining

  [ ] Electric Utilities

  [ ] Energy Conservation

[ ]

Health Care

  [ ] Biotechnology

  [ ] Health Insurance

  [ ] Hospitals & Physicians

  [ ] Pharmaceuticals

  [ ] Other Health Care

[ ] Manufacturing

Real Estate

  [ ] Commercial

  [ ] Construction

  [ ] REITS & Finance

  [ ] Residential

  [ ] Other Real Estate

[ ] Retailing

[ ] Restaurants

Technology

  [ ] Computers

  [ ] Telecommunications

  [ ] Other Technology

Travel

  [ ] Airlines & Airports

  [ ] Lodging & Conventions

  [ ] Tourism & Travel Services

  [ ] Other Travel

[ ] Other

☐ Environmental Services

☐ Oil & Gas

☐ Other Energy

5. Issuer Size

Revenue Range   OR   Aggregate Net Asset Value Range

☐ No Revenues   ☐ No Aggregate Net Asset Value

☐ $1 - $1,000,000   ☐ $1 - $5,000,000

☐ $1,000,001 -   ☐ $5,000,001 - $25,000,000
$5,000,000

☐ $5,000,001 -   ☐ $25,000,001 - $50,000,000
$25,000,000

☐ $25,000,001 -   ☐ $50,000,001 - $100,000,000
$100,000,000

☐ Over $100,000,000   ☐ Over $100,000,000

☒ Decline to Disclose   ☐ Decline to Disclose

☐ Not Applicable   ☐ Not Applicable

6. Federal Exemption(s) and Exclusion(s) Claimed (select all that apply)

☒ Investment Company Act Section 3(c)

☐ Rule 504(b)(1) (not (i), (ii) or (iii))   ☒ Section 3(c)(1)   ☐ Section 3(c)(9)

☐ Rule 504 (b)(1)(i)   ☐ Section 3(c)(2)   ☐ Section 3(c)(10)

☐ Rule 504 (b)(1)(ii)   ☐ Section 3(c)(3)   ☐ Section 3(c)(11)

☐ Rule 504 (b)(1)(iii)   ☐ Section 3(c)(4)   ☐ Section 3(c)(12)

☒ Rule 506(b)   ☐ Section 3(c)(5)   ☐ Section 3(c)(13)

☐ Rule 506(c)   ☐ Section 3(c)(6)   ☐ Section 3(c)(14)

☐ Securities Act Section 4(a)(5)   ☒ Section 3(c)(7)

7. Type of Filing

☒ New Notice   Date of First Sale ☒ First Sale Yet to Occur

☐ Amendment

8. Duration of Offering

Does the Issuer intend this offering to last more than one year? ☐ Yes ☒ No

9. Type(s) of Securities Offered (select all that apply)

[X] Equity	[X] Pooled Investment Fund Interests
[ ] Debt	[ ] Tenant-in-Common Securities
[ ] Option, Warrant or Other Right to Acquire Another Security	[ ] Mineral Property Securities
[ ] Security to be Acquired Upon Exercise of Option, Warrant or Other Right to Acquire Security	[ ] Other (describe)

10. Business Combination Transaction

Is this offering being made in connection with a business combination transaction, such as a merger, acquisition or exchange offer?   [ ] Yes [X] No

Clarification of Response (if Necessary):

11. Minimum Investment

Minimum investment accepted from any outside investor $0 USD

12. Sales Compensation

Recipient	Recipient CRD Number [ ] None
UBS SECURITIES LLC	7654
(Associated) Broker or Dealer [X] None	(Associated) Broker or Dealer CRD Number [X] None
None	None
Street Address 1	Street Address 2
1285 AVENUE OF THE AMERICAS	

City	State/Province/Country	ZIP/Postal Code
NEW YORK	NEW YORK	10019

State(s) of Solicitation (select all that apply)
Check "All States" or check individual States   [X] All States   [ ] Foreign/non-US

13. Offering and Sales Amounts

Total Offering Amount $400,000,000 USD or [ ] Indefinite

Total Amount Sold $0 USD

Total Remaining to be Sold $400,000,000 USD or [ ] Indefinite

Clarification of Response (if Necessary):

The general partner of the Issuer reserves the right to offer a greater or lesser amount of limited partner interests. The Total Offering Amount and Total Remaining to be Sold are aggregated together with the Issuer and its related parallel fund.

14. Investors

☐ Select if securities in the offering have been or may be sold to persons who do not qualify as accredited investors, and enter the number of such non-accredited investors who already have invested in the offering.

Regardless of whether securities in the offering have been or may be sold to persons who do not qualify as accredited investors, enter the total number of investors who already have invested in the offering: [0]

15. Sales Commissions & Finder's Fees Expenses

Provide separately the amounts of sales commissions and finders fees expenses, if any. If the amount of an expenditure is not known, provide an estimate and check the box next to the amount.

Sales Commissions $0 USD [X] Estimate

Finders' Fees $0 USD [X] Estimate

Clarification of Response (if Necessary):

Placement agent fees to be paid based upon a fee schedule. Such fees are offset dollar-for-dollar against the management fees payable by the Issuer.

16. Use of Proceeds

Provide the amount of the gross proceeds of the offering that has been or is proposed to be used for payments to any of the persons required to be named as executive officers, directors or promoters in response to Item 3 above. If the amount is unknown, provide an estimate and check the box next to the amount.

$0 USD [X] Estimate

Clarification of Response (if Necessary):

The general partner is entitled to a performance allocation. The investment manager is entitled to a management fee. The performance allocation and management fees are fully disclosed in the Issuer's confidential offering materials.

Signature and Submission

Please verify the information you have entered and review the Terms of Submission below before signing and clicking SUBMIT below to file this notice.

Terms of Submission

In submitting this notice, each issuer named above is:

- Notifying the SEC and/or each State in which this notice is filed of the offering of securities described and undertaking to furnish them, upon written request, in the accordance with applicable law, the information furnished to offerees.*

- Irrevocably appointing each of the Secretary of the SEC and, the Securities Administrator or other legally designated officer of the State in which the issuer maintains its principal place of business and any State in which this notice is filed, as its agents for service of process, and agreeing that these persons may accept service on its behalf, of any notice, process or pleading, and further agreeing that such service may be made by registered or certified mail, in any Federal or state action, administrative proceeding, or arbitration brought against the issuer in any place subject to the jurisdiction of the United States, if the action, proceeding or arbitration (a) arises out of any activity in connection with the offering of securities that is the subject of this notice, and (b) is founded, directly or indirectly, upon the provisions of: (i) the Securities Act of 1933, the Securities Exchange Act of 1934, the Trust Indenture Act of 1939, the Investment Company Act of 1940, or the Investment Advisers Act of 1940, or any rule

18. Dominion shares an address with Smartmatic in Barbados (see below)

19. Dominion data is seen going to their headquarters in Serbia and Toronto.

20. The following link analysis was gathered through open-source methodologies and is easily verifiable.

21. As Dominion and Smartmatic makes claims that they are not connected in any way, not only are they connected but their business registration was in the same building on a foreign island to obfuscate their business dealings.

https://offshoreleaks.icij.org/nodes/101732449

1. The following link analysis was gathered through open source methodologies and easily verifiable.

2. As Dominion and Smartmatic makes claims that they are not connected in any way, not only are they connected but their business registration was in the same building on a foreign island to obfuscate their business dealings.

https://offshoreleaks.icij.org/nodes/101732449

https://offshoreleaks.icij.org/nodes/101724285 Dominion Certificates

SMARTMATIC INTERNATIONAL CORPORATION

Connected to **1 address**
Connected to **13 officers**
Connected to **1 intermediary**

📅 Incorporated: 29-SEP-2004 ❶
◉ Registered in: Barbados
◉ Linked countries: Barbados

🅰 Data from: Paradise Papers - Barbados corporate registry
❶ Barbados corporate registry data is current through 2016
🔍 Search in opencorporates
🔎 Got a tip? Help ICIJ investigate: contact us or leak to us securely

ICIJ OFFSHORE LEAKS DATABASE

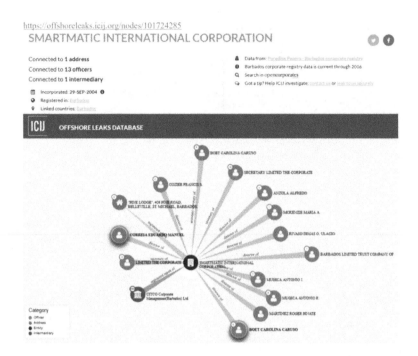

Dominion Certificates

Dominion can be seen using open source methodology that the SSL certificates from *.dominionvoting.com were registered on the 24th of July 2019. This SSL certificate were used multiple times from locations ranging from Canada, Serbia, and the United States. These images verify that Dominion systems were connected to foreign systems across the globe. Also seen is

25. Dominion can be seen using open-source methodology that the SSL certificates from *.dominionvoting.com were registered on the 24th of July 2019. This SSL certificate were used multiple times from locations ranging from Canada, Serbia, and the United States. These images verify that Dominion systems were connected to foreign systems across the globe. Also seen is that the SSL certificate is used for the email server that was the same for the secure HTTP connections.

443.https.tls.certificate.parsed.fingerprint_sha256:
8f73a14d5f0fc10ebfa3086a99b9e7a550e822c71d762e627b73d12
e5f1b8b9c

that the SSL certificate is used for the email server that was the same for the secure HTTP connections.

443.https.tls.certificate.parsed.fingerprint_sha256:
8f73a14d5f0fc10ebfa3086a99b9e7a550e822c71d762e627b73d12e5f1b8b9c

All share:

443.https.tls.certificate.parsed.fingerprint_sha256:
8f73a14d5f0fc10ebfa3086a99b9e7a550e822c71d762e627
b73d12e5f1b8b9

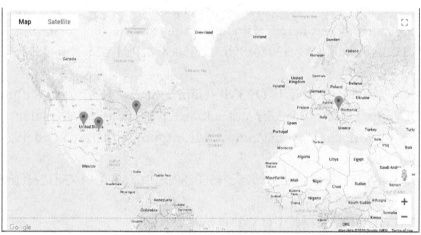

Email ip address: 206.223.168.94
Serbian ip address 82.117.198.54
Dominion site 204.132.219.214
Cloudflare link 104.18.91.9
Canadian ip address 206.223.190.85

Denver ip address 204.132.121.11

Page: 1/1 Results: 7 Time: 155ms

206.223.168.94 (webmail.dominionvoting.com)

BEANFIELD (21949) Toronto, Ontario, Canada

443/https

*.dominionvoting.com, dominionvoting.com

443.https.tls.certificate.parsed.fingerprint_sha256:

8f73a14d5f0fc10ebfa3086a99b9e7a550e822c71d762e627b73d12e5f1
b8b9c 82.117.198.54

SERBIA-BROADBAND-AS Serbia BroadBand-Srpske Kablovske
mreze d.o.o. (31042) Kac, Vojvodina, Serbia

443/https

*.dominionvoting.com, dominionvoting.com

443.https.tls.certificate.parsed.fingerprint_sha256:

8f73a14d5f0fc10ebfa3086a99b9e7a550e822c71d762e627b73d12e5f1
b8b9c 204.132.219.214

CENTURYLINK-US-LEGACY-QWEST (209) United States

443/https

*.dominionvoting.com, dominionvoting.com

443.https.tls.certificate.parsed.fingerprint_sha256:

8f73a14d5f0fc10ebfa3086a99b9e7a550e822c71d762e627b73d12e5f1
b8b9c 104.18.91.9

CLOUDFLARENET (13335) United States 443/https, 80/http,
8080/http Direct IP access not allowed | Cloudflare *.dominionvot-
ing.com, dominionvoting.com 443.https.tls.certificate.parsed.finger-
print_sha256:

8f73a14d5f0fc10ebfa3086a99b9e7a550e822c71d762e627b73d12e5f1b8
b9c 104.18.90.9

CLOUDFLARENET (13335) United States

443/https, 80/http, 8080/http Direct IP access not allowed | Cloud-
flare *.dominionvoting.com, dominionvoting.com443.https.tls.certifi-
cate.parsed.fingerprint_sha256:

8f73a14d5f0fc10ebfa3086a99b9e7a550e822c71d762e627b73d12e5f1
b8b9c 206.223.190.85 (206-223-190-85.beanfield.net)

BEANFIELD (21949) Toronto, Ontario, Canada

22/ssh, 443/https *.dominionvoting.com, dominionvoting.com 443.https.tls.certificate.parsed.fingerprint_sha256:
8f73a14d5f0fc10ebfa3086a99b9e7a550e822c71d762e627b73d12e5f1 b8b9c 204.132.121.11 (204-132-121-11.dia.static.qwest.net)

CENTURYLINK-US-LEGACY-QWEST (209) Denver, Colorado, United States 21/ftp, 22/ssh, 443/https, 80/http DVS Fileshare *.dominionvoting.com, dominionvoting.com 443.https.tls.certificate.parsed.fingerprint_sha256:
8f73a14d5f0fc10ebfa3086a99b9e7a550e822c71d762e627b73d12e5f1 b8b9c

Kavtech

26. A Pakistan based Business Intelligence firm with ties to the ISI.

27. The lead data scientist named Bilal Khan Nawabzada tweets directly to ISI.

28. The Co-Founder Waqas Butt is cc'd on emails containing personally identifiable voter information from the Nevada Secretary of State.

  a. This is a similar and deliberate act of unauthorized access of information and data as the hacking of the voter registration system by Iran. (E.O. 13800 of May 11, 2017)

29. Kavtech is a Pakistan based Business Intelligence firm with ties to the Pakistani intelligence ISI. The lead data scientist named Bilal Khan Nawabzada directly references Pakistani ISI in his social media.

30. Kavtech using Natural Language Processing and Sentiment Analysis to sway Voter opinion and intent to ultimately influence the election.

Kavtech

- A Pakistan based Business Intelligence firm with ties to the ISI.
- The Co-Founder Waqas Butt is cc'd on emails containing personally identifiable voter information from the Nevada Secretary of State.
- The lead data scientist named Bilal Khan Nawabzada tweets directly to ISI.

Fwd: Your Nevada Secretary of State Eligible Voter List Report

---------- Forwarded message ----------
From: <DataTransfer@sos.nv.gov>
Date: Sun, Nov 29, 2020 at 9:54 PM
Subject: Your Nevada Secretary of State Eligible Voter List Report
To: <Roberta@truethevote.org>
Cc: <waqas@kavtech.net>

Your report results for report "Eligible_Voters_15_July_2020" has been generated and is ready to be downloaded from https://www.nvsos.gov/yourreports/VoterList.35923.112920195210.zip. If you can not click this address, just cut and paste this address into your web browser's

Bilal Khan Nawabzada @bilal_... · Jun 8
'There is no power on Earth that can undo Pakistan'' and ISI has always proved it.
#YesIamISI

    ⟲   ♡ 2

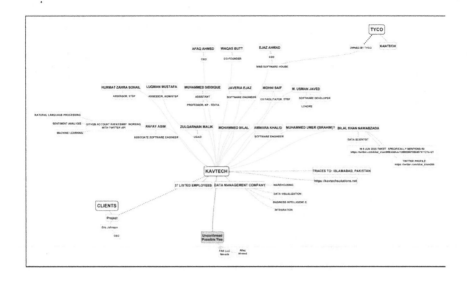

Supply Chain Concerns

31. One in five components used in voting machines are from China-based companies

32. On January 6, 2017 DHS Secretary Jeh Johnson on the Designation of Election Infrastructure as a Critical Infrastructure Subsector.

a. This means that election infrastructure becomes a priority within the National Infrastructure Protection Plan. It also enables this Department to prioritize our cybersecurity assistance to state and local election officials, but only for those who request it. Further, the designation makes clear both domestically and internationally that election infrastructure enjoys all the benefits and protections of critical infrastructure that the U.S. government has to offer. Finally, a designation makes it easier for the federal government to have full and frank discussions with key stakeholders regarding sensitive vulnerability information.

33. With that in mind, it is incredible that the Election equipment used in the November 3, 2020 election was manufactured in Russia, China and undisclosed Asian and European Countries (see below).

Phases and Participants in a Supply Chain for Election Equipment for Use in the United States

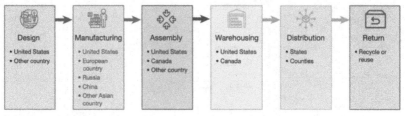

SOURCE: The countries listed are found in Interos, 2019.

Reference:

https://us-cert.cisa.gov/sites/default/files/2020-10/AA20304A-Iranian_Advanced_Persistent_Threat_Actor_Identified_Obtaining_Voter_Registration_Data.pdf

https://www.whitehouse.gov/presidential-actions/executive-order-imposing-certain-sanctions-event-foreigninterference-united-states-election/

https://www.jstor.org/stable/resrep26524seq=13#metadata_info_tab_contents

https://www.dhs.gov/news/2017/01/06/statement-secretary-johnson-designation-election-infrastructure-critical

----

[END OF STATEMENT]

What you have seen thus far was generally prepared by or before Thanksgiving, November 26, 2020 by my colleagues, the dolphin-speakers and analysts.

Let us now turn to an analysis of the packet traffic on Election Day 2020 provided me by the best cyber-forensics specialists I have ever met. I cannot reveal the source of this right now beyond saying that. And that, while there is some small piece of the public who has a guess what the source is, I say: I know what is publicly known about this source, plus some additional information not known to the public but which adds, along with adding to the credibility of this data. So I know what the public knows plus a little bit more, and what I know is enough that I believe this data can be presented to the public, with such disclaimer as I have just made. Here is what the public needs to know:

As packets travel through the Internet they leave a trail, and dolphin-speakers using the right tools can, in a sense, "shine a light" and reveal those packet trails in the cyber-fog. The cyber-specialists to whom I refer have access to such tools (and even more arcane ones), and have documented vote-flipping in the Problematic 6 states amounting to 299,567 votes, just enough in each state to flip the election. 43% of that activity came from China.

For those who wish to study the data behind this claim, here: US Election Fraud 2020_General

For those who shudder at the thought of opening an Excel spreadsheet, this *1 minute video* graphically depicts how, on Election Day, hundreds of foreign entities (many in China) were conducting Man-in-the-Middle attacks on election system across these states of Pennsylvania, Michigan, Wisconsin, Arizona, Nevada, and Georgia to flip votes.

Foreign Interference

The first lesson we learn in 5th grade civics is, "Just law derives from the *consent of the governed*," and how we find out what it is to which *we*, the *governed*, in fact *consent*, is to hold elections that are free, fair, and transparent. It is the atomic concept of our intellectual tradition.

In my view, any reasonable person who looks at the constellation of facts and articles and videos and data I have presented so far will say, "There is enough about Election 2020 that smells like skunk that we need to dig deeper." And any who looks at that constellation and says "Nope, I see nothing, NOTHING!" is either Sergeant Schulz, or gas-lighting.

So if the game, Dear Reader, was to show enough evidence to bring you to an adequate threshold of doubt about Election 2020 before I continue with my narrative, I hope that I have shown you enough to win.

Chapter 4: How the Crisis Could Have Been Ended Fairly & Quickly

I have covered the subjects of why I was learning about election fraud in the months preceding November 3; irregularities in the November 3, 2020 election that matched what I had been warned might occur; and evidence of foreign entanglement in some of these irregularities. Now I turn to the subject of what I was hoping to have done. I am going to do that now so as not to leave the reader in suspense, and so that the reader might accurately judge the subsequent actions I took, and decisions I made along the way.

What is it I thought should be done? By the middle of November it was clear to me that we as a country were facing a Constitutional novelty: I knew by then that Election 2020 was an egg that could not be unscrambled. In 6 swing states there had been an unknown amount of election fraud (but apparently industrial in scope, which we could show with access to ballots and hard drives). There was no way to unravel all the effects of the cheating and figure out what the pre-fraud numbers would have been. Yet the other side of recognizing the fact that the election was *industrially* fraudulent in those states, was to recognize that the election results from those locations were 0% trustworthy and could not be fixed.

That analysis left what seemed to me the only reasonable course of action one could take. As I saw it, the path least injurious to the Constitution was this:

> **The Plan**: Let's look at the six counties where mass irregularities occurred. These machines were sold to the public with the promise, "there is always a paper ballot fail-safe." Hold them to it. There is an Executive Order that says, should foreign nations interfere in an election, the

President has extraordinary power to straighten it out. Let him direct a federal force to go to those counties and open up the boxes with the paper ballots, and count them, on live-stream TV. If there are not big discrepancies, Trump concedes. But if there *are* big discrepancies, we would re-run the election in those six counties, or states, using that federal force. Yes it would be a bad precedent, but so would trying to force down the public's throat an election that had been rumbled by goons in six key cities, and about which between 33% - 47% of the population has significant doubts. That's not healthy for democracy, either. I figured the initial live-streamed reread of the ballots in six counties would take 3 days, and (if called for) the election to be re-run in those six states, in 30 days.

What federal force would be right? I favored a combination of US Marshall Service and National Guard. The country needs to trust the result, and those in military uniform enjoy the highest trust level from society. In addition, the National Guard ("Our sons and daughters and co-workers.... Our Citizen Soldiers") live among us. However, it could have been the DHS, the FBI, the DEA. But the counting would have to be federal, and shown on livestream from each counting operation.

Which is why in early-mid November, as tensions started to escalate, I was hopeful that brisk action could be taken. The results would create an outcome where President Trump would either say, "No big discrepancies, fine, I concede". Or he would say, "See, there were discrepancies in the hundreds of thousands of votes in each of these locations. We are re-rerunning the election in those states using the National Guard." If undertaken with dispatch, the first matter (a federally-supervised livestream recount) might have been resolved in about three days; if discrepancies appeared, the rerun of the election might even have been resolved in time for normal operation of the Electoral College on December 14.

That's it. That was the plan. It went through various elaborations, various nice-to-haves, but at heart that is all that was sought by myself and the team of Cyber-ninjas with whom I was working. That is all that was needed. The alternative was accepting a highly irregular national election that would divide our nation for years. That is why I say, "This was a 3-foot putt. Maybe easier." Seems rather tame and reasonable to me (though I suspect we are entering an era where the thought-control goons will label the plan I just described as, "extremist").

We could have resolved this Constitutional crisis in days or weeks. I think it would have been far less injurious to the Constitution than what has happened instead: an election whose integrity is doubted by 47% of Americans, has been shoved down the throat of America, and in order to prevent any future backsliding, the Goons are considering sedition laws that tell roughly half the population that they are terrorists. That is *also* insulting to the Constitution.

I think it is clear, in retrospect, that the solution I described would have left us with more confidence in our government than we have today.

Yet I get ahead of myself. I have explained, Dear Reader, what brought me into this subject and what I learned about it before Election Day (November 3), what I learned might happen, how what *did* happen matched the predictions, and the data and evidence we surfaced in the month of November concerning domestic irregularities in the election, as well as signs of foreign involvement. I made clear how I read the evidence. Lastly, I have explained what we were fighting for, what it was that myself and my fellow-travelers wanted to happen, the course I tried to hip-check our country into taking (whene'er a chance I got) as the weeks and ultimately two months unfolded. Lastly, I argue it was a less extreme path than the path that has been taken, which may include the government implementing police-state style laws on the grounds of stopping extremists.... such as people who see anything strange about any of this.

So now you know where I am coming from in the story that follows. Those were the grounds of my suspicions and the course of action I thought would minimize injury to the Constitution while doing our best to sort out an election that had been hopelessly compromised. "It is an egg that could not be unscrambled", I wrote then, believing that once that truth was recognized, the plan that I proposed made the most sense.

For all I know, that point of view may be called "extremist" today or tomorrow.

Now I shall now rewind and pick up a parallel narrative. This parallel story starts about a week after the election (November 9?) with a cyber-ninja and I walking into an office building in suburban Virginia, just outside of DC. We had a still fragmentary yet already compelling reconstruction of what had happened on November 3 and the days immediately following it. We had the crime about half-solved, and what was remaining seemed almost a mechanical matter: dig here, compare this with that, see what answers spit out. *We can see they were doing this this and this, but you also need to look into that.*

I and my cyber-sleuth colleagues walked into that building to take a meeting with Sidney Powell, Esq. (esteemed lawyer for Michael Flynn, the "Peoples' General"), and with America's Mayor, Rudy Giuliani.

Chapter 5: All the President's Teams (November 9 – December 17)

I will refrain from saying too much about my relationship with Sidney Powell. For one thing, it started off with me walking in with information, but over time it became something like I was working for her, helping her get answers to her questions. Then, if I recall correctly, she became my lawyer. Whichever it was, the relationship became something for which privilege surely applies. One cannot selectively waive privilege, and just share things one *wants* to share while claiming "privilege" on the others. I know that. But I can say is that our relationship started with me walking in off the street as a volunteer with information, and so I can talk about that phase of the relationship, but in time it became formal enough I will not be able to say more.

Mayor Giuliani, however, never became my lawyer, and I will not be so constrained in my accounts. My ultimate purpose (my only real purpose) is to deliver to the public as honest a rendering as I may construct of the events between November 3 and January 20. It seems like a historically worthy thing to do.

For my part, though they thought of me as an entrepreneur, I introduced myself to them as the proprietor of this website, Deepcapture.com. I pointed out that back in 2008 it had won numerous awards for its business investigative journalism and had also been voted the best journalism regarding corruption within the United States. I may have done other things in life, but in addition I'm a journalist, and I have the rights any journalist has. This means I can investigate what I want to investigate, I don't *have* to reveal how I learn things, and if I feel like sharing some of my findings with lawyers like Sidney and Rudy, it is no different than the dozens of other times this website has investigated things and shared its findings with lawyers, or even with law enforcement.

That first meeting I had with Sidney lasted 45 minutes. When I arrived at the office a strange hum hung in the air, as it does when people have just had words. I found Sidney sitting by herself in an empty space on one side of the office building. We got to business: Sidney was well-informed, open-minded, and on top of things. We had an intelligent conversation.

Sidney was in touch with people from the earliest days of the creation of these systems, and soon she showed that her information covered a portion of the narrative about which we had *some* knowledge but not much (mostly concerning the origin of the machines and their reason for certain design flaws). On the other hand, as we ran through what my side of the table had already teased out of the data in the days since the election, Sidney showed she understood what we were saying, and we quickly tied together what we each knew. It was a highly-productive first conversation, and she ended it by telling me that I needed to go to the other side of the office, find Rudy Giuliani, and tell him everything I had just shared with her.

So my cyber buddy and I went to the other side of the office building, to Rudy's side, which I understood to be the center of gravity of the operation.

I will explain what I expected to find. I expected to find something like what we had created (as I described in previous chapters): A command post staffed by quants and cyber-ninjas and lawyers. The quants would be doing statistical work, driving answers to feed lawyers being notified of such irregularities as I have walked through previously, and would be availing themselves of whatever remedies the law surely provided. I figured there would be a war-board, with the states in question having boxed out all relevant data, progress, and to-do's. There would be an information loop, obviously, such that the campaign headquarters in each state would be on a daily conference call to receive updates on progress. Thinking that may be a fair bit for one 76-year-old gentleman to manage, I imagined Rudy might have some strong COO, perhaps a lawyer, or perhaps an executive, who might be keeping assignments on track.

What I found was this:

The place was 20% empty, and another 30% were packing out their desks.

One conference room held a number of lawyers around a table. At least three of them were solid. These lawyers were each assigned one or more states. Yet there were things going on at the state level and below, local lawyers were jumping in with actions of their own. Things were bubbling up organically without direction or cooperation from this group in Virginia. I came to learn that between Rudy's legal team and the campaign staff there was zero communication (even though they jointly occupied an office story). And between Rudy's legal team and the campaign staff and those local groups and their lawyers, there was zero communication. I did not know at first if that was for a legal reason or just the way they operated. In time, I saw it was the latter.

> **The Mediocrity** – I do not wish to be mean about it. For example, I am not going to reveal the gender or other details of this person (other than to say: imagine a person who is a lawyer and who had once had a career at one of the better-known government agencies). But given how deliberately horrible to work with, and destructive Mediocrity's behavior was, I will refer to the person as, "Mediocrity".

> **The Commish** – Think of Mike, from *Breaking Bad*. The quintessential cop. Tough, correct, and courteous, but poker-faced and dead-eyed at all times. Sits in meetings with hand casually

covering his mouth, saying nothing. When asked, *might* open his mouth, and if he does he invariably has something intelligent to say. In fact, it is so intelligent it is rather creepy, because it makes one wonder, "Why does he work so hard to keep his opinion to himself?" He's the one guy who should be talking, but he rarely does.

The Mayor – Rudy Giuliani. I spent the late 1980's in a hospital in New York City, and remember occasional Mafia killings outside Brooklyn joints or a mid-town steakhouse (it was good for business, they'd say). Rudy was US Attorney there and then, breaking up the Mob. I always felt an affinity for him because of that overlap in time and place. And of course, on 9/11, Rudy became "America's Mayor". We intersected a few times in the years after that, but when we crossed paths he never indicated he remembered me. His security company handled an issue for me when I was fighting Wall Street. I doubt he remembers, but when he ran for President in 2008 and came through Utah, local Republicans called me and asked to introduce Rudy at a gathering in a large Utah home. I studied up on him, drove over, and gave a short introduction on Rudy Giuliani to the crowd, lasting about 30 seconds. Rudy took over, we shook hands, and that was my sum contact with Rudy Giuliani in his political days.

I always remembered something from the Q&A that impressed me. A question on abortion came from the staunchly pro-life crowd. Rudy answered, "No, I'll never support a law that criminalizes abortion for the woman. Laws on abortion have always been directed at doctors, not mothers. I'll never put a woman in jail for having an abortion. If that is what you folks are looking for, I'm not your man." He lost 2/3 of the audience but gained the respect of 1/3, among them myself, simply out of respect for such rare directness.

Twelve years later, at 3 PM on an afternoon about a week after the election, I walked into the office space being shared by the Trump campaign and the law firm springing up around Rudy Giuliani to investigate and challenge election irregularities surfacing from the 2020 election.

As indicated above, it was nothing like what I expected to find: data-gathering feeding loops driving decision-making to keep a large and geographically distributed workforce operating successfully. Law firms are notoriously poorly-managed businesses in any case, they truly are, but the law firm-campaign space that had taken shape within that office was a particular shit-show. People wandered vaguely from meeting to meeting. The meetings I saw were run like bull sessions, with no agenda, no format, and no apparent sense of urgency.

Within 45 minutes I was ushered to a room where I was to have 30 minutes with Rudy. Physically he was more of a grandfather than I remembered, a bit less robust, a bit more hunched, a bit more irascible. I explained to him the outline of what we understood at that point, an outline such as the reader might have after reviewing the cascade of stories regarding porous security in election systems cited above, as well as the presentation by MIT Math Ph.D. Dr. Shiva, or the exposition by Seth Keshel. I feared overwhelming him, so I tried to simplify. As I spoke he occasionally grunted stoically, so it was difficult to judge what was sinking in. After about 10 minutes Rudy started checking his multiple phones for texts, right in front of me, as we sat together. Or conversing with one of his assistants, sending someone on a side errand, or receiving a report back. It felt strange to be talking to a man who was paying so little attention, but the Commish, sitting on the side, motioned for me to continue. After 30 minutes I was ushered out of the office, but told to hang around.

Eventually, I was brought back into a smaller room with Mayor Giuliani, and again asked to explain what happened. Realizing I may have overwhelmed him with my earlier explanation, and gotten lost in the forest for the trees, I broke it down simply and slowly, like one would for one's 76-year-old Grandfather. Again within 5-10 minutes he was fidgeting, grunting on occasion, sending people on side errands, checking his multiple phones for texts, and typing responses.... Meanwhile, I tried to stay on track.

There was a moment 15 minutes into the meeting when I got a whiff of something in that small office.... Medicine? Booze? Just as I was taking a sniff to determine, someone rushed in with some unrelated issue, and I was escorted from the office.

Again I wandered around among the staff, most of whom were professing to know nothing about what was going on, and many others of whom were packing up their desks into bankers' boxes. Given what I already knew about the Deep Rig by that point, I was perplexed and found myself drifting around the convoluted office space. 30 minutes later I was strolling outside some other conference room down the hall when I heard Rudy's familiar voice saying, "...don't understand a goddamn thing this guy's saying..." drifting out of a doorway. Startled, I looked around the corner, and there was Rudy talking to whatever group of staffers happened to be sitting in that conference room to which he had moved.

Several staffers pulled me aside in a hallway. *What Mayor Giuliani is going to need*, one told me, *is a one page summary. Very simplified.. A one-pager.*

Another piped up, *And bulletpoints! The Mayor likes bulletpoints!*
Mediocrity added, *But with graphs and data.*
But no more than one page! Repeated the first.

At the risk of sounding snobbish, I was insulted by Mediocrity and these 20-something staffers giving me writing advice, and such asinine advice at that. I told them I would have something in 48 hours. I requested one favor: any other requests that came from them should be orchestrated through *one* of their people, who would call *one* person whom I would designate among my colleagues, and that way we would have structure, and keep track of deliverables as we accommodated their needs so that it would not all turn into a shit-show.

I left and drove back to DC. By evening there were three open requests from three different people on Rudy's team for my colleagues. One of Rudy's people wanted to handle requests of *this* type, one only wanted to handle requests of *that* type... And the shit-show began.

Before I continue with my story, however, I wish to be clear that I do *not* claim that everybody in that large but melting office space was incompetent. As I said, there were three smart, competent, skillful lawyers (a fourth if one counted a Constitutional law scholar who was in-and-out). Yet the atmosphere was one of despair, staffers were wandering around in the dark, and the meetings seemed like sophomore bull sessions rather than anything organized and disciplined.

From contacts with several staffers over the weeks that followed, I learned what had happened just before I arrived that first day. Rudy had declared to the lawyers including Sidney, "You can never prove election fraud in a courtroom!" He insisted it was not going to be part of their legal strategy. Instead, the strategy was to challenge the election in various states on procedural grounds: *In this state this one county had this set of rules, this other county in the same state had that a different set of rules, that violates the Equal Protection Clause of the 14 Amendment.*

So I was correct: just before I arrived there *had* been a blow-up between Rudy Giuliani and Sidney Powell, ending with Rudy shouting at Sidney in condescending, vile and profane terms that caused Sidney to walk out in front of an office of multitude people. Rudy declared that none of this was going to be about election fraud, and he put his staff of lawyers to work on procedural filings.

Later, a member of Rudy's team told me that initially, Rudy had not even wanted to do that much. He had wanted to make three more-or-less token challenges in three states, then call it a day. Sidney's insistence that he was missing the Big Picture had caused Rudy to relent and allow a somewhat more aggressive posture to be taken. But still, nothing was to be about election fraud or the possibility of a rigging of the election. Rudy could tolerate hearing about a couple of hundred dead people in Philadelphia voting, but he did not want to hear about anything more sophisticated than that.

That afternoon in early November, the first time I arrived in their building nearly a week after the election, I had stumbled in on Sidney just as she walked out of that exchange. And Sidney had sent me to talk to Rudy because she needed someone else to explain what she herself realized: a new form of election fraud had emerged that was not about *hundreds* of dead people voting in a city, but was about the possibility of *several hundreds of thousands* of votes being injected into each of several locations. Rudy had not been processing any of it from Sidney, and probably did no better from me, and that was why he kept trying to talk about how Joe Frazier (1944-2011) was still voting in Philadelphia.

Over that weekend, Sidney sent a brilliant female junior attorney over to sit with me and a few of the dolphin-speakers . That junior lawyer had anticipated staying 30 minutes, but after an hour and a half she went into the next room and called Sidney. She told Sidney that we had the goods, or at least a well-developed understanding of what had gone on in various states, and even specific counties.

From that point forward our relationship with Sidney was perfect. As we researched and made discoveries, we brought them to her and her staff, and they would listen closely, patiently, and ask intelligent questions. Then they began incorporating the material into their pleadings.

That being the case, I will say no more about how Sidney and I worked.

Mark Twain once ended a long letter to a friend by writing, "If I'd had more time I would have written you a shorter letter." In those two days after meeting the Mayor I had the time to draft what his staffers had requested, and 48 hours later I was putting the finishing touches on as simplified a one-page summary as I could create. My aim was to pare the story down until the Mayor could not lose the forest for the trees, and the Mayor would grasp the entire narrative in a succinct one-page bullet point read. At that point, once he understood the Big Picture, we could begin diving in on each sub-claim: data and affidavits would be adduced, and so on.

But to begin with, Rudy needed to absorb a one-page briefing (in fact it was 80% of a page), into which I had distilled the research of a team of people who had been sniffing down a half-dozen different alleys. It was concise and clear. I included a second page of one graph, concerning one state, backing up a claim made in that one-pager: once Rudy got it, I thought, once we agreed where we were, I would supplement with additional graphs for the other relevant states. Affidavits that were being gathered would be adduced to document each of the other claims made. And so on and so forth. But this time we were going to crawl, walk, run.

At 11 PM I got a phone call telling me Mayor Giuliani and entourage were dining in such-and-such a Georgetown restaurant, and would I mind bringing what I had written to them. I got dressed and went, but when I arrived his security told me to wait in the bar. I did for 45 minutes until someone came from the Mayor's private dining room to tell me the Mayor asked that I not come back to his table (security was concerned about me, apparently), but asked me simply to send into the private dining room the paper I had written. I sent it in, then left.

Later, people in that room told me what happened when my paper arrived.

First, in the 90 minutes between 11:30 PM and 1 AM, Mayor Giuliani imbibed three triple scotches on ice. Those relating this story could not vouch for what he had drunk before 11:30.

Second, Rudy read my paper for 20 seconds, then put it aside saying, "I'll get to this later."

Third, the Mediocrity was at the table. The Mediocrity picked up the one-pager Rudy had set down, and holding it between thumb and forefinger like it was a turd, announced with a laugh, "Can you believe Byrne worked two days on this and this is all he wrote?"

Nine hours later Rudy Giuliani took the stage at a joint press conference held with Sidney Powell and Jenna Ellis. Rudy was meant to give a situation report then introduce Sidney Powell, who was going to discuss the possibility of mass election fraud on a scale no one was yet comprehending. That it was not about a couple hundred dead people voting *here*, or a few hundred illegal votes *there*, but about something deeper, systemic..... Unprecedented.

Instead of sticking to the plan, Rudy Giuliani got carried away, and huffed and puffed for 40 minutes about how many hundreds of dead people had voted *here* and how illegal people had voted *there*... *And Joe Frazier still voted! How does a dead person vote? Would you tell me that?* As Grandpa worked himself up, repeating all the same points he had been making for days, hair die ran down both sides of his face.

Nine hours earlier he had thrown back nine shots of whiskey in 90 minutes.

Another story that came to me from those times within Rudy's offices: One Pennsylvania lawyer, a female, had taken the job of preparing a filing in Pennsylvania. She received a message from opposing Kirkland & Ellis counsel that was so unprofessional, so threatening, that *Kirkland* later had to withdraw from the case. She also received a death threat. Shaken, the female Pennsylvania lawyer sent her draft filing to Rudy's team, but she withdrew her representation.

Rudy had had to find a firm, overnight, that would finish the Pennsylvania filing. He found a lawyer in Texas with election experience who finished it and got it filed in Pennsylvania. It made no mention of election fraud and was instead focused on the procedural Equal Protection arguments. Rudy only read it on his way traveling to the Pennsylvania court where he was to defend it: upon reading it, he told his companions. "*This is the worst piece of shit filing I've ever had to stand up in a courtroom and defend.*" He went into that Pennsylvania courtroom and was destroyed. Here is a partial transcript:

> Matthew W. Brann, U.S. District Judge: *So it's correct to say then that you're not alleging fraud in the amended complaint?*

> Rudy Giuliani: *No, your honor, it does not, because we incorporate by reference in 150 all of the allegations that precede it, which include a long explanation of a fraudulent, fraudulent process, a planned fraudulent process.*

> Judge: *I understand that. So the amended complaint, does the amended complaint plead fraud with particularity?*

Rudy: *No, your honor, and it doesn't plead fraud. It pleads the, it pleads the plan, the scheme that we lay out in 132 to 149 without characterizing."*

We got a call from Rudy's team that we needed to have a set of computer forensic specialists down in Georgia the following morning. They would be provided access to a set of voting machines they could "exploit". The licensed and certified computer forensic people with me demanded answers, such as, *Where are the machines? What kinds of machines are they? Tampering with election equipment being a federal felony, under what legal authority will we be operating? Will there be law enforcement there to review and document all actions taken, for any chain-of-evidence questions that might later arise?*

The response from Rudy's team was, "We've got all that covered. Get down to Georgia, *stat!*"

With misgivings, I caused the requisite people to fly into Georgia from various locations. They were driven to a precinct where, it turned out, someone had indeed vaguely promised that access would be given to machines.... But that person was not there that day. Or had changed his mind. The dolphin-speakers sat around then were driven to another precinct where, this time, they were told there would be someone with a court order granting them access to certain machines. No such person was there, but a group of hostile county employees was. Again they sat around waiting for Rudy's lawyers to arrange paperwork, but nothing arrived. After hours of waiting in the parking lot, in the early evening, they drove away, and as they sat at a traffic light a half-mile down the street they saw 17 police cars, light-bars flashing, go rolling by on their way to the building my cyber-buddies had just left. My pals quickly and safely returned to their respective home states.

Over the next month and a half, a number of my colleagues interacted with Rudy from time to time, afternoons, evenings, and weekends. Nearly all mentioned two things: the amount of attention he was paying to his daily podcast, and his drinking. His own staffers joked with us about it.

Those who were around him knew: almost every evening, Rudy was toasted. That, and his podcasts, were the only guarantees in Rudy's life.

In that first week after the election, we had fashioned an operation of some kind. We had cyber-ninjas and quants before November 3. But by a few days after the election, we had so many volunteers, plus many witnesses and whistleblowers and people with relevant stories seeking us out, and so many were flying to DC to find me, that we had to set up operations in hotels scattered around the city. From our volunteers with a background as military officers we found our debriefers, and created a system where they were privately and professionally meeting with witnesses and whistleblowers, listening to their stories, and crafting summaries. These were being fed up into a chain of analysts who were jockeying those pieces together with information coming together from our cyber guys and other sources, and building a picture of increasing granularity of what had happened on November 3-4.

In the months before the election General (ret.) Michael Flynn and I had met telephonically. We had known *of* each other for years, as there is a strange connection between us, a deceased man who had played a role in both of our lives decades past. Conversing with Mike was like meeting and speaking with another entrepreneur: we finished each other's sentences and saw what needed to be done almost without conversing. At some point he arrived on the scene, and I told him in detail about this assemblage of talents that had come together in various ways: the cyber guys, the quants, the flow of witnesses and affiants into our circle, our structure of multiple debriefers, our information-flow back up to a circle of analysts putting everything together. I had rough-hewn the whole structure expecting General Flynn's arrival, with the understanding that when he arrived, I would be handing the keys to it over to him. He seemed pleased with what we had accomplished within a week of the election.

General Flynn suggested we relocate the HQ of that structure to a location far away from DC, far away from any city, in fact. Information was bubbling up from those networks around the country, through the capillaries of the debriefers and report writers, and into a central organ: I thought of it as "the liver". Mere yards away, there would be an office full of lawyers acting as the legal intake for the information we were pulling up. In short, we were still in the process of spinning up the structure, and we needed to plug into the lawyers who would be playing legal chess. *We agreed that both Sidney and Rudy would get all output from this structure.*

Everyone relocated to the location selected. There was a team of lawyers in place there. However, around them there were a variety of people with no discernible roles and who gave me the creeps. One ex-Agency female, a large, loud woman, and not a lawyer, suddenly became quite the unbidden organizer. Another participant, a cocky Englishman with a military background, suddenly announced that he was gatekeeper between this room and that. It all began giving me quite a nasty feeling. But after only two days I got word from Flynn: things having been stood up and roughed-out as we had agreed, Flynn asked me go back to DC to start speaking to the public. We agreed we would cross paths for 30 minutes in a certain location as we switched places.

I got ready to leave. I asked the Brit to pass on three key messages to someone I was not going to have a chance to see before leaving. He agreed. I said each one simply, and he nodded curtly after each. When I was done I asked him if he understood. He said casually, "Yep. Got 'em all."

"OK, please repeat them back to me," I told him. He stared at me, unblinking. "You say you got them, so repeat them to me." He could come up with nothing. He had not actually listened to a word. I told him to get a pen and paper and make three notes. He did so begrudgingly.

For some reason, I was supposed to take the ex-Agency woman back to DC with me. We drove to the location at which Mike Flynn was arriving. Once there, the female slipped off to the side and told someone that she had learned something that meant she had to stay behind. Flynn arrived, and we had 30 minutes on a tarmac together. We caught up, synched up. I told him that I had misgivings about a British guy who was at the camp, and about the ex-Agency woman who was hovering around me. Then I left.

The next day, back in DC, I received the word: the ex-Agency woman had made up a lie to get permission to stay, but it had all unraveled on her. It had something to do with something I had asked her to do or had asked her not to do, or some research, or something: whatever it was, it was a fabrication (barely a word had passed between us), designed to get herself turned around and reassigned to stay in that operation in the countryside. They also confronted the cocky British guy, and though I think he never broke, I am told he was implicated in the minds of everyone there. Security walked both characters off of the premises. After their departure, suspect wiring was found in the crawl space of the house.

This is not to say that all time was being wasted. The structure of information flow I described, the one that had self-organized (and I helped rough-out a bit), was taken over by a three-star General who had had a career in Military Intelligence, and he made it far better. He organized the people and made sure they had what they needed to do their jobs. Soon it was spitting out refined analyses that began informing the briefs Sidney Powell was writing. We made sure that everything that was generated was also provided to Rudy.

That is the background to presentations such as ones I have been referencing. Again, for an excellent example, watch Seth Keshel, here. Seth is a former Army Captain (Intelligence) and played a key role in that structure I just described. Seth is a quirky guy, a poly-sci junky, certainly on the spectrum, and just all about the numbers. That link goes to a 21-minute video that provides an excellent example of the kinds of work that was being done within the structure that I have described above. For a good understanding of the type of work that was being done, you should watch at least a portion of this.

Doug Wade Interviews Seth Keshel

Other examples of the kind of work we were doing can be found replicated in the parallel work of others who went public. For example, the clear-speaking mathematician Edward Solomon gave two public presentations, one dissecting Georgia's results, one more general. The patterns and puzzles you see Solomon unraveling in these two videos were precisely what our own cyber-ninjas were doing inside our group:

Edward Solomon - Geometric Proof for Georgia

Edward Solomon Videos · Published February 7, 2021 · 25,536 Views

Edward Solomon - Geometric Proof for Georgia
And this excellent 50 minute presentation also:
Smoking Gun: ES&S Transferring Vote Ratios between Precincts in PA.
- By: Edward Solomon

Back in DC, rejoined with my cyber-colleagues, we became aware of a disconnect we could not seem to fix. The Mediocrity had evolved into our point of contact with Rudy's team, and nothing seemed to flow well. On November 26, Thanksgiving Day, we were all sitting together in a restaurant in DC, and discussing their problems. Sitting there eating turkey dinner, they gave me quite an earful. How the Mediocrity was super-controlling about information, plans, access. How the Mediocrity seemed to think they were peons, and was telling them, "Go here, go there," with no explanatory information, no sense of "Hey teammates, this is what is going on, and we are going to work on it together!" One key player on the team was warning that he would quit if he had to have any interactions with Mediocrity again.

I had trouble believing the stories they were telling me. Among them were some horrible ones concerning Mediocrity's proclivity for hitting on people of the opposite gender, and possibly the same gender, in ways that were embarrassing to all present (the Mediocrity had asked one of my married colleagues to meet one evening, and when the hotel door opened the Mediocrity was in underwear, waiting). But now it was boiling over, they told me, because they had received an order that they were all to be in Antrim, Michigan in two days. Again, Mediocrity would answer no questions about where exactly they were going, exactly what machines they were expecting to find, under whose authority would they be opening machines and imaging hard drives, even how long would they be there, should they arrange their own rental cars, etc. None of it was explained. Mediocrity had just sent word to be in such-and-such a place in Michigan, *stat!*

Then, life being life, we looked up, and there was Mediocrity strolling through the DC restaurant not far from our table. We caught each other's eye, and Mediocrity came towards us. Thinking it was a nice opportunity to pour oil on troubled waters, I received Mediocrity gracefully, intending to converse in front of my colleagues civilly, and get things back on track.

Soon talk turned to Michigan, and I was asked would I be able to get the right people there at the appointed hour. Thinking it might be a moment of management development, I suggested, "You know, with requests like these, it would help us to be better informed. My colleagues would like to know things like, 'Exactly where will they be going? Are the people there going to be cooperative? What kinds of machines might we be exploiting? What legal authority is enabling them to image one of these voting machine hard drives? Will there be rental cars provided?' You know, just the basics before people get thrown on another mission like what happened in Georgia."

"Look," the Mediocrity said, standing over us at late Thanksgiving Dinner. "First, what is your corporate structure?"

We all looked at each other, male, female, 75, Weaponized Autism and others, not previously having given the matter much thought. We were just a bunch of people who had found each other and were trying to expose what looked like a world-historic election fraud together. Finally I said, "Our corporate structure is that we're the Bad News Bears. I'm team coach."

"Ok Patrick," Mediocrity continued. "Here's what's up. I've told you where your people need to be in Michigan on Saturday. Be there. Or tell us you cannot, and we'll find someone who can."

In my astonishment I began to respond, and to my further astonishment, the Mediocrity began speaking over me. "I'm telling you where you need your team to be. If you can't handle it-"

I used something I had not used in a couple decades, something I had seen an economist professor friend do to another professor, a Lefty, who had continuously interrupted him (as Lefties are want to do in place of having good arguments). I just started speaking, "Well it may sound like I was finished speaking but I actually wasn't and while you might think you are going to speak over me actually I am just going to continue talking like this until you pipe down and I did not care if it takes all night because I know that it may have sounded like I was finished but actually I wasn't and......" and so on and so forth. Without a break. For about 10 seconds until the Mediocrity got that I was serious, and was just going to continue speaking like that until Mediocrity shut up. Which eventually the Mediocrity did, looking somewhat astonished, having evidently gotten away with such behavior in decades of federal employment.

Then I politely said, "Where in the *fuck* do you get off? We don't work for you. We're volunteers offering to do things you have no clue how to do. Go find someone else anytime you want. The way you people work in this city is astonishing. If you ever try to work at a modern company like Google, or Facebook, your ass will be fired in a New York minute. You *suck*."

I surprised myself, because I do not normally speak that way to people, but I did that time. Perhaps it was three weeks of frustration boiling over. I said that conversations with Mediocrity were constant games of narcissist deflection, how amateurish Mediocrity was, how anyone walking around saying things like "Either you do this or I find someone who will!" and "Failure is not an option!" is a mediocrity who may have learned management within government but who if ever moved to the private sector would get fired by noon. When making such requests of my colleagues, any competent person would provide relevant information. Fill them in on the mission, let them brainstorm, they'll be able to contribute....

I saw Mediocrity was crestfallen, and realizing I had overdone it, I gently escorted Mediocrity from the table. I tried to put a nice façade on things, so as not leave Mediocrity embarrassed. As we parted, Mediocrity turned to me and said, "Don't worry. I'll be with the President. I'll make sure you get full credit for all of this."

Exasperated, I returned to my seat. Minutes later we saw that Mediocrity had, in fact, been part of a larger party, and walking out was none other than Mayor Giuliani. I quickly sidled up to him. It was 10:30 PM, his step seemed unsteady, and I went to his elbow like one would escorting Grandpa to a taxi. I told him, "Sir, this is not going well with your colleagues. May I respectfully request a way I might contact you directly, so we can keep things on better track?" The Mayor pulled out his cell phone and had me take his number.

In that weeks that followed I called and texted that number on a half-a-dozen occasions. Not once did Mayor Giuliani respond to me.

Over these weeks I got to know several excellent White House staffers. Smart young men and women in their late twenties or early thirties, generally. Some (but not all) were Trump enthusiasts. They filled me in on details here and there, snippets of what was happening behind the scenes among the campaign, Rudy, and the White House. One evening, once we were close enough, I let down my hair and said, "This is a shit-show. Is this .... normal?" One of the staffers (and mind you, a pro-Trump one) said, "This is the Trump White House. This is how everything has run for four years."

The Bad News Bears got where they needed to be in Michigan, when they needed to be there. Mediocrity was there, along with staff from Rudy's team. They went to the expected precinct and like Georgia, it was a bust. The machines were not what we had been led to expect. No real authorities were there, or law enforcement, or warrants: just a mildly cooperative 75 year old lady working in a public building that had acted as a voting precinct.

While the Mediocrity hung around chatting up county workers of the opposite sex, the dolphin-speakers went to work. It turned out the 75 year old lady who ran the place had a story about how, on the day after the election, some people from "County" had shown up and instructed her to insert her card and re-run her machine using some different inputs. What she was saying did not make sense, and it was clear that someone had taken advantage of an elderly woman who probably does not send her own texts. Finally she mentioned that, unbeknownst to County, she had kept both the paper audit trail of the original run, and the re-run, and had stored them in a closet. Our geeks got excited, and had her bring them out: they unrolled them on a long carpet, and in a few minutes of study, they began finding things. Alarming things.

The Bad News Bears got the Mediocrity to break away from Coffee-Klatch With The Deputies, and pointed out what they were finding in the paper audit rolls. Finally they suggested, "You are a lawyer, right? Don't you think you should be getting some affidavits here?" Startled, "Oh yes, of course," scrambled Mediocrity, and did so, getting affidavits from the 75 year old lady and one or two other employees who had the useful information.

Those learnings and those affidavits were fed to a Michigan lawyer who was pursuing his own election fraud case in Michigan. Days later a judge read it, and found it alarming enough that he gave a court order for a formal exploitation of the Antrim County voting machines. The Bad News Bears returned to Antrim County and this time, with a proper court order in their pocket, they were able to image hard drives, and returned to base camp with those images. By working in staggered shifts around the clock, over the next four days they performed a month's worth of work, first breaking the security on the imaged hard drives, then reconstructing the files, then analyzing them. That was all fed up through the system, and emerged about a week later as an eye-opening report that created a national stir, known as the Antrim County Computer Forensics Report.

BOMBSHELL: Antrim County Computer Forensic Report

December 14, 2020 · 3 sec read

You wanted the evidence. Here is the evidence.

antrim_michigan_forensics_report_121320_v2_redacted

You can read it for yourself, but I will share one detail: the Dominion voting machine audit logs were erased on the evening of November 4, 2020. There were audit logs on the machine for 2018 and previous election years, but those for 2020 had been erased. That should tell you all you need to know, but read the full report if you wish.

Other things were happening nationally. Some concerned federal employees had been tracking events in a certain Western state and were sure they knew how vote flipping was being done there. The problem was, when asked to allow inspection, the relevant judge (a Democrat) would insist on stalling for a couple days, thus giving time for the opposition to go in and do a "smash-down" (a hacker's term for fixing evidence after-the-fact, in anticipation of an audit, making sure everything ticks-and-ties correctly). But they made a mistake in one location, and their smash-down failed. The data that turned up was so telling, so indicative of fraud, that the lawyers went back to the judge arguing it provided grounds for a far more sweeping order that would let them examine machines across the state. The judge agreed in principle but suggested that the precinct needed to have that data verified again before he could use its discrepancies to justify such a sweeping order. The concerned federal employees put the location in question under observation, and sure enough, that night there were three cars in the precinct parking lot. They were redoing their smash-down so that this time it would work. In the morning the data was fixed, and no further orders were coming out of that judge.

However, unbeknownst to all, the concerned federal employees in question had recovered enough material both to document the original, and the smash-down. They also got the license plates on those three cars: they tracked back to a left-wing union which shows up repeatedly in the background of events of recent months.

Meanwhile, back in DC, I was hearing things out of Rudy-World. I heard that he was getting paid $20,000/week, and there were those claiming he was just "mailing it in" for a paycheck. However, later I was told that Rudy was working for free, and the $20,000/day bill had been a billing error from an uninformed assistant. I do not know what the truth was.

More importantly, from others in Rudy-world I began hearing the number "$207 million". The claim was that the Republican Party had raised $207 million to "stop the steal". In one version it grew past *300* million. In one version of the staff rumor, the finger on the button for those millions was a high-level woman at the Republican National Committee. In another version, it was being jointly managed by that RNC woman and the Commish, and they were definitely keeping an eye to the future. In everyone's version of the story, $100 million had been set aside for future legal defense. But whoever was in charge, they were sitting on the money, and I never saw a penny of it being spent in any way to "stop the steal".

So I say to whatever Republican loyalists around the country coughed up those hundreds of million, in donations of $10 and $20.... You were fleeced. It was a big joke: rank-and-file Republicans gave a pot of hundreds of millions of dollars to Republican Bigshots to unscramble what had happened on November 3, and from where I sat, nothing went to any activity related to doing so. It was all being stashed by people at the top, licking their chops. Rudy promised money to fund Matt DePerno – the Michigan patriot who took on Antrim County on his own, but he never came through.

In Georgia, there was a faction that had been in touch with me from days after the election. This was an especially interesting network of people with law enforcement and quasi-law-enforcement backgrounds. Since November 4 they had been reverse-engineering the Rig there in Georgia. They had put people and locations under observation, and had filmed a variety of activities through telephotos. They mapped and tracked numerous parties involved, and even tracked the organizers down to a small element, a Leninist cadre, who were staying in a motel together and managing the Deep Rig around the state of Georgia. For their own reasons this network needed to stay in the shadows, yet as the weeks rolled by, they were providing good information, helping us reconstruct what had happened in Georgia. What our cyber-ninjas and quants and analysts were getting out of *their* methods matched what was being reported by this network of people with many boots on the ground.

The fight in Georgia became surreal. There was an earnest young man who was both a staffer for a Senator and dating the daughter of the governor. His car exploded in an apparent accident (see "BIZARRE EXPLOSION CRASH IN GEORGIA – KILLS HARRISON DEAL" December 5, 2020).

BIZARRE EXPLOSION CRASH IN GEORGIA – KILLS HARRISON DEAL

December 5, 2020

An apparent car crash in Georgia – kills Harrison Deal. He was a staffer for Georgia Senator Kelly Loeffler. Harrison Deal was also dating Gov Kemp's daughter.

It was on a 4-lane highway, it was sideswiped by another car, then it blew up. The engine flew 75 yards.

Fiery 3-vehicle crash on Interstate 16

Most videos of the accident have been removed from the internet, but some remain, and show a car burning in a fireball: it was quite an ornery car accident.

Then the Georgia Bureau of Investigation got involved. Three days later, the officer conducting the investigation committed suicide.

Meanwhile a Georgia election worker named Ruby Freeman made a video boasting of committing massive criminal fraud in her election work. Ruby is the mother of the woman videoed yanking large amounts of ballots out of hiding and scanning them multiple times in a Georgia voting station that was "shut down" and had had all observers removed on the false claim of a pipe busting. In Ruby's social media posting, she takes credit for committing precisely the election fraud that we were claiming occurred.

Ruby Freeman Fraud Videos

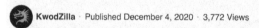

KwodZilla · Published December 4, 2020 · 3,772 Views

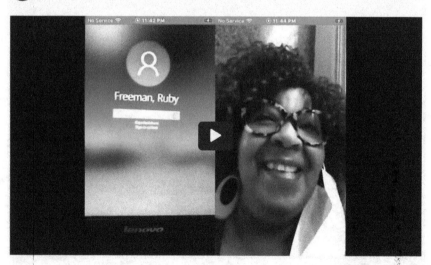

Ruby Freeman Fraud Videos

In her online confession to election fraud, she expressed precisely the attitude that, I maintain, was held by enough people to make rigging a national election possible:

Add   VeritasS..
election should be ordered immediately.

💬 498   ↻ 8 991   ♡ 42,9K   ⌁

↻ Carol Czarkowski retweeted

Nik🏳️ 👋 ⌐ @mermazingnik · 18h
This is Ruby Freeman's confession of voter fraud!! Let's make her famous!!
#RubyFree   ctionFraud
#voterfraud   heSteal2020

+ —   196 rumbles   EMBED ↗

Rumble — Ruby Freeman - Screengrab of confession to Voter Fraud Crime

Ruby Freeman - Screengrab of confession to Voter Fraud Crime

Ridiculous video footage continued to emerge, shredding the possibility of seeing this election as one that measured the will of the people, or could be unscrambled so as to discover it.

CAUGHT: Surveillance footage shows GA poll worker scanning the same batch of ballots MULTIPLE times!

CAUGHT: Surveillance footage shows GA poll worker scanning the same batch of ballots MULTIPLE times!

A technologist and inventor named Jovan Pulitzer went public regarding his technologically-oriented investigations into the Georgia election. Jovan's approach was to look past all the different *theories* as to how the election had been scrambled, and simply do a forensic audit on the ballots, determining which had actually been folded and mailed. For the cost of half a million dollars, we could have run a million or two million ballots in Georgia, and had a forensic audit complete in a few days. Everything could have been settled simply and quickly. Here is a short video of Jovan explaining his idea:

MUST-SEE: Jovan Pulitzer EXPOSES MASSIVE FRAUD in Georgia Election

Meanwhile, even moderates in the public space who were researching for themselves were stating the obvious: "When Math in Public is for the Republic: *Want evidence about election fraud? Here's some. I'm tempted to call it proof.*"(November 29, 2020)

Over those weeks, Rudy scheduled hearings in some states. His plan had evolved to getting enough evidence in front of state legislatures that they would go off automatic pilot and begin making hard decisions. Most of these hearings were unofficial, conducted out of rented hotel spaces. His star witness was the Colonel from military intelligence with whom I had been working since August, 2020, who was brought to these different states to report and synthesize the information that the Bad News Bears were surfacing. He did an able and convincing job, but we all began to wonder: *What's the strategy here? Is there a strategy? Rudy's strategy (if there is one) seems to be just a long march through the courts. Taking cases to the states and appellate levels. Imagining he is going to win by running the tables through the court system. Or getting state politicians to do something brave.* But that was not going to work, as the courts are ponderous anywhere, especially disinclined to get involved in election matters, and were already setting court dates out past January 20. And politicians do not do brave things. Yet Rudy just kept plodding along with an occasional hearing and of course, has a daily podcast. It did not make any sense.

Along the way, the same Goons that had been normalizing political violence in our domestic discourse since June, 2020 began to feel emboldened. Here, a Wayne County election official named Monica Palmer initially refused to sign off on the results for which she was to certify, on the grounds of the kinds of affidavits, statistics, and forensic evidence then accumulating. Palmer was immediately denounced as (what else) "a racist" and her children's lives were threatened.

Here is the Goon who did that:

The will of the people will not be silenced.

Rumble — All to get what he wanted. Which was her vote changed in the vote certification. That's illegal right?

"Abraham Aiyash doxxed Monica Palmers children, announcing names & school then called her a racist"

Oddly, such explicit violent intimidation of an elected official began passing almost without comment or official response. If the violence threatened was from the Left. For example, here is a Michigan State Rep Cynthia Johnson menacing the lives of political opponents. Grading on a curve for 2020 that may perhaps seem not too odd, until one realizes this was not an off-hand remark, but a calculated comment she recorded and put up on YouTube. That she thinks it appropriate under any circumstances tells you something about the times in which we live:

Rumble — Michigan Democratic State Rep. Cynthia Johnson threatened Trump supporters in a Facebook live video Tuesday, saying it is a warning message to those who support the president.

Rep Cynthia Johnson Threatening trump supporters

I believe that it only took a small number of such incidents to do grave damage to our nation. Political violence (from the Left) was normalized. My colleagues and I started seeing it in our whistleblowers, the people from around the country who were in contact with us who were giving or considering giving affidavits on their experiences. It certainly had a chilling effect on them, and several requested temporary protection. Some received it.

Mike, Sidney, I, and others developed a Solution-in-a-Can. It was really the solution we had started within in mid-November, redone by a top-notch lawyer and a 3-star General. Under various orders signed previously by both Obama and by Trump, if an election had foreign entanglement, the President had a broad spectrum of powers. The President on his own judgement could sign a "finding" saying that there was adequate evidence (e.g., the report authored by the FBI and CISA, not to mention other information that I have related) of foreign involvement on numerous fronts, which arguably would have justified a vigorous response. However, we had only a narrow, tailored on in mind: based on the information that had been turned up, the President should use his powers under the requisite Executive Orders to send US Marshalls and the National Guard into the six problematic counties, open up the paper ballot backups, **and recount them on live-streamed TV** (those sitting at home because of Covid could follow along). Ideally, they would also image the hard drives of (but leave in place) the election equipment in those counties, for forensic examination.

If there were *no* big discrepancies, Trump would concede.

If there *were* big discrepancies, such as half-a-million vote discrepancies that we suspected might fall out, then more aggressive courses of action could be countenanced, such as re-rerunning the election in those counties or states. The recount of the six counties could be easily done in a week, and if it justified further action, the entire resolution could still be achieved on a Constitutional timeline.

Either that, 47% of the electorate had to choke down an election whose integrity they doubted.

General Flynn drafted a beautiful operational plan for such a mission. One signature from the President and the whole thing would roll. The teams would be created from the right National Guard Units, the right directives to each... A more expansive version of the plan had recounting conducted in 17 counties around the nation, Democrat and Republican, including the Problematic 6. That expansive version of the plan envisioned paper ballot recounting plus imaging of hard drives of these voting machines for further forensic analysis (but not "seizing" the machines: they were to be left in place, and just have hard drives imaged).

There were weak and strong versions of the plan in other ways. An uber-expansive version of the plan would have had the paper ballots not just *recounted* but *forensically audited* (but we thought that was too much to ask for with the possible exception of Georgia). However, in a pinch, we could hit just the Problematic 6 counties, and even simply recount the boxes of paper ballots. We' have a preliminary answer in 2-3 days, thus ending a great deal of national drama. And it need not be done by the National Guard: US Marshalls and DHS and/or FBI might make up the federal force.

Mike and Sidney had the legal research, the draft finding, the general's Execution Checklist that would, upon Presidential signature, make everything run like a Swiss watch.

And yet, things slid and slid. Rudy went off to organize a hearing in a hotel room and wanted one of our people there to speak.... Days spent waiting for warrants that never came.... Absolutely no sense that there was anyone *with* a plan, let alone *executing* one. We saw the Constitutional deadlines beginning to loom...

The days turned into weeks. December came. Somewhere in those weeks a grizzled and retired Navy Master Chief was on the scene for a few afternoons. His summary of Rudy's operation was memorable: "It's like watching a half-dozen monkeys trying to fuck a football." The simile struck me as incredibly apt. Imagine walking into a zoo, seeing a cage with six monkeys in it, tossing a football inside, and watching them all try to fuck it. There'd be screeching and snarling and fighting and running around.... and none of the monkeys would make any progress towards the goal. So that Master Chief's phrase seemed spot-on, and really tickled my funny bone.

Then it was mid-December. Yes we had state matters spinning along, yes we had geeks inspecting packets and finding foreign interactions, yes we were finding that the registration of every new Nevada voter was transmitted to Pakistan ISI, yes we were finding machines with wireless cards in rooms with smart thermostats that had been breached from overseas, yes we were learning why live voting rolls were kept overseas..... But Flynn and I had a sense our side was chasing its tail. That opposition was running out the clock. And Rudy's approach would allow that.

At one point I learned how the President was staying involved. It turned out the answer was: periodically, Mayor Giuliani and Mediocrity were going over to the White House to brief him. Really, no kidding: the person who was so bad my colleagues had declared they would quit rather than work another moment with that person, and the 76 year old guy who had trouble sending an email and was doing podcasts and getting sloshed, were the ones explaining to the President the cyber-crime of all time and what his options were. At first I thought it was a sick joke, but I confirmed it. The Mayor and Mediocrity were the point-people on the mission of addressing this world-historic event.

There were times that Flynn and I confessed to each other that we felt sick. A frequent subject of mutter between us ran along the lines, "Why the fuck are we doing this?" The president's children were off, uninvolved, pep-rallying, or planning their retirements. We could detect no discernible strategy out of the President's team, no marching orders, just an organization wandering around in circles and melting as it did so. A person who was so bad, we had had to make special arrangements such that Mediocrity did not have contact with our Bad News Bears, or they were going to flee. And the whole mess was led by a 76 year old gentleman, a man beloved by all including myself, but who six weeks into what might be the most sophisticated cyber-theft in all of history, still could not have a coherent conversation beyond, *Did you hear that 211 dead people in Philadelphia voted? Dead people?!?!? And they voted! Joe Frazier voted! He died in 2011 but he voted! Have you heard?!? How do you vote when your dead?!?*

And then we would remember why we were doing it: America's brand is "elections". It is what we do. We had a national election that appears to have been compromised in a remarkably strategic way, it shows the hand of foreign involvement, it may be part of a Chinese psyop to take over our country, and there may never be free, non-goon elections in America again. We'd often remind each other, *That's* why we are not supposed to quit.

And that is why, a week before Christmas, General Mike Flynn, Sidney Powell, and I decided it was time to take a chance. By hook or by crook we were going to Jedi-Mind-Trick our way into the White House, maneuver our way to the Oval Office, and get the President's attention ourselves. With no invitation from him.

Chapter 6: Crashing the White House (December 18-22)

On the evening of Friday, December 18, Sidney Powell, Mike Flynn, a sharp female attorney on Sydney's team (whom I will call "Alyssa"), and myself decided to call an SUV and be driven near the entrance of the Eisenhower Executive Office Building, which is on the grounds of (and connects to) the White House. We had a vague plan regarding how we were going to get through all the rings of Police, Secret Service, and Marines: Sidney and Mike were the center of global attention, and we were going to try to use that to bullshit our way through and get to the Oval Office. Beyond that, we'd be playing it by ear (I *did* say the plan was "vague").

There was a fine young NSC staffer whom I had gotten to know who, a real *mensch*, and I called him and left a message that I was accepting the open offer he had extended to drop by his office anytime, and was coming over ... right then. At 6:15 PM. Sidney asked another excellent staffer to work on a parallel course. Not knowing if they would play ball, we may have been less than clear about our intentions.

We were dropped off a block from the security gate and walked through the light snow falling in the darkness. We got to the first security booth, and when the Police and Secret Service saw it was Sidney and General Flynn

("The People's General"), they stiffened to attention. My staffer buddy came out from inside, and when he saw Flynn and Sidney he froze and looked at me with raised eyebrows. I gestured that we were all together, and he looked shocked for a moment, then strode over to the guard, flashed his ID, and asked him to let us all in. With muted relief the guards quickly said, "Take care, General" and we were through the first layer.

For the second layer my staffer-buddy and one of his fine colleagues joined us as we walked into the inner ring entrance, and spoke for us: again, when they saw Mike the guards again all stiffened to attention, then briskly and professionally processed us all through quickly. They were silent and asked no questions. I was the last one through, and as they handed my ID back to me one leaned in and said quietly and intimately, "Thank you Mr. Byrne." I was surprised, and it was the first I understood that in the constellation of Michael Flynn and Sidney Powell, there was a faint little star of my own.

We were ushered inside to an office, to use as Base Camp. If I recall correctly, we were in Base Camp for about 30 minutes before making a move for the office of another staffer, another young and principled person, with an office closer to the Oval Office. Camp 2.

Once there, Mike Flynn made contact with someone with whom he had worked in his brief stint as National Security Advisor, someone with an office that could serve as Camp 3, from which would come the final assault on the summit (the Oval Office). "Hey yes it's Mike, how you've been? ..... Oh my Gosh, so great to hear your voice too..... Yeah yeah, it was unbelievable.... Where am I? Oh actually I'm in the White House! Yeah, just came by to see ... See me? Sure well how about I just swing by... sure sure see you in a moment."

We launched for Camp 3. And sure enough, when we got there, as Mike Flynn stood talking to his former colleague, Sidney and I had a 20 foot line of site into the empty Oval Office......

After a few minutes, through a private door on the far side, Donald Trump walked into the Oval Office. He was dressed in a creased blue suit and tie, still, at 7:30 PM. He glanced out the doorway to where Sidney Powell and I were already walking towards him, greeting him like he was expecting us. President Trump's eyes knitted in puzzlement but he recognized us, and after just the briefest hesitation he beckoned us in. Within seconds General Flynn, Sydney Powell, and I were all sitting in the Oval Office with President Donald J. Trump, with the door shut behind us.

So that happened. Really.

The President sat across the Resolute desk and made small chat with Mike, asked how he'd been. It had been four years since they had seen each other (when Flynn left the White House weeks into Trump's first term). He asked after Sidney as well. I gave and received no more than a nod, letting Mike and Sidney take the lead. As I have noted publicly, the first thing I noticed about him was how measured, gracious, and even soft-spoken Trump seemed to be, so unlike the character that has beamed at us for years through the media.

Eventually he glanced at me again, raised an eyebrow, and gave a small chuckle. Apparently, he knew about me, as I thought might be the case. He said something quietly, civil and kind. I said, "Thank you Mr. President..." He cocked his head quizzically and said something about knowing that I had not voted for him, and had said a number of critical things of him. I let him know the truth, that I had said some harsh things before the 2016 election, but while he was President my estimation of him had grown, and that in any case none of it was relevant, that I was there because I was confident the election had been rigged. I told him, "We think there is a much shorter route through all of this than your team is pursuing."

I closed adding, "But Sir, entrepreneur to entrepreneur, I feel I must mention something. As you may know, I have been swimming around outside of your administration for a couple of months now, and I must tell you, I do not think you are being well-served by many people in the White House. I can bring in young staffers who will tell you that your senior leadership doesn't want you to win. They want you to concede."

The President raised his eyebrows at my frankness. Then, like a man who knew the answer, he quietly asked, "Why?"

"I'm not sure," I said, "but I hear people are getting signals that if they're good boys and get you out the door, there will be jobs waiting for them. But if they don't, they won't be getting offers from the right law firms, they won't be getting invitations from the right country clubs, they won't be getting invited to the socialite parties on Manhattan..." Trump grimaced, and we moved on.

Sidney and Mike began walking the President through things from our perspective. In brief: there was a quick way to resolve this national crisis because he had power to act in ways he was not using. Under an Executive Order that he had signed in 2018, and another Executive Order that President Obama had signed in 2015, he could "find" that there was evidence of foreign interference with the election. Doing so would give him authority to do *big* things, but we were going to ask him to do one *small* thing: direct a federal force (we suggested US Marshall Service + National Guard) to go to the six problematic counties in question and, on live-stream TV, re-count the paper ballots that were held as fail-safe back-up. It would only take a few days. Even better would be if they imaged the hard-drives and those images could be examined forensically (which would make the project last no more than a week, as we had already cracked the Antrim County machines and knew precisely what to do going forward).

In either case, if there were no mischief found, then President Trump would concede the election. But if (as we suspected) evidence of tens or hundreds of thousands of improper votes was found in the six counties in question, then he would have a wide variety of options. He might have those six *states* re-counted on live-stream TV. Or he might have *50* states re-counted on live-stream TV by federal forces, and America would finally have its answer to, "How much election fraud goes on in our nation?" Or he might skip that and have the National Guard re-run the elections in those six states. We pointed out that, it being December 18, if he signed the paperwork we had brought with us, we could have the first stage (recounting the Problematic 6 counties) finished before Christmas. And even if the result was sketchy enough it demanded a rerun of the election in those states, it could be done before January 20, so that the January 20 Constitutional deadline would not be disrupted. The more time that he let slide by, the more compressed things would become. If he waited to see what the January 6 outcome was, however, and then decided to follow a plan such as ours, it would engender accusations of "sore-loserism", so he had to act quickly.

The alternative was an election that 47% of Americans doubted, which would not be good for the country.

After absorbing the plan, the President said, "You know Pat," he said to me, catching my eye and giving a little snort of humor. "You know, I could leave here and my life would be really .... fine. I could be with my family, my friends, I could be playing golf ..." We looked at each other and shared a moment as may occur only with CEO's and other "leaders": people think our lives are glamorous, but in many ways they suck. I had a flashback: *the first time I was running a firm, a 24-person manufacturer of industrial torch tips in New Hampshire, I went on a sales trip to Europe. Some colleagues (engineers) and I spent a couple of weeks crawling around on plasma machines in a shipyard in Spain, a crane manufacturer in Belgium, knocking on factory doors in Hamburg, then attending a gigantic conference in Essen so we could walk around getting business cards and grabbing people to sit with us for a bagel to hear a sales pitch because we could not afford our own booth, but we needed a big order so we could make payroll the next quarter. After a few weeks of it we were home to New Hampshire, being received by colleagues like we were jet-setting royalty. "Oh Spain! How was Spain? Belgium! Germany!... Gosh I always wanted to travel, what was it like?" That's when I realized that people do not understand that the CEO life is not as fun as people think, dreaming of taking it easy, of being able to take a walk without worrying about the (in my case at the time, dozens, in Trump's case, hundreds of millions) of people depending upon you.*

I understood why Trump was chuckling, and I nodded and chuckled along with him. I got just what he was hinting: he was thinking that from a personal (74 year old's) standpoint, leaving the White House, going to Florida, and golfing had *real* appeal. "So Pat, on January 20 I could walk to Marine One and climb aboard and go have a really good life...." He continued, talking softly to me, directly. "But this? Knowing I was cheated, that they rigged this election? How can I just walk away from that?"

Other than that, of that first 30 minutes we had alone with the President, most of the conversation was among the President, Mike, and Sidney, so I had a lot of time to study President Trump, and I was surprised on many fronts. When he questioned Sidney's legal reasoning that he had the power to do such a thing, she pulled out the Executive Order he had signed in 2018 and described one from Obama in 2015. Trump took the E.O. and scanned it quickly, then began asking pertinent questions from it. The same with the finding that he would need to sign: he asked questions of both Sidney (regarding legalities) and Mike (regarding substance), who discussed with him the kinds of information regarding foreign interference covered in the last chapter. Throughout it all what I saw was a strong executive mind, taking in information quickly and calculating decision-trees. It takes a lot to impress me, but what I saw was a sharp mind in action. It surprised me how I had seen no mention of it in four years.

Finally, Trump stopped and scanned the three of us, and asked simply. "So what are you saying?" Thinking of the difference between the highly organized, disciplined approach I had experienced with Flynn and Sidney, versus the college sophomore bull-session approach of the Campaign and Rudy-World, I spoke up again: "Mr. President, I think you should appoint Sidney Powell your Special Counsel on these election matters and make General Flynn your Field Marshall over the whole effort. If you do you'll win. I know Rudy's your lawyer and friend, and he can have a great role in this. Rudy should be personally advising you, and we don't want to do anything to embarrass him. But Sidney needs to take point legally on this, and if you want to be sure, make General Flynn here Field Marshall. If you do your chances are around 50-75%. You should see how well Mike has this planned, it would run like clockwork..."

The President shook me off, saying, "No no no, it's got to be Rudy."

After some time (20-30 minutes?), three lawyers appeared together. They did not introduce themselves, and huddled in the back of the Oval Office, listening. In addition, Mark Meadows and someone else joined us by speaker phone. Eventually the lawyers in the back began muttering things to make their displeasure and disagreement evident. Finally President Trump said something indicating this was new to him, wondering why no one had shown him this route through the impasse. I said again, "Sir, again, CEO to CEO, you are not being served well by those around you in the White House. I've gotten to know staffers in your White House, and they tell me they are being told that leadership here is telling them to get you to concede."

Trump started to say something to Mike and Sidney, but he stopped himself and turned back towards me. "Who?" He asked angrily, "Who wants me to concede?"

I was taken aback by his anger, as I thought it was common knowledge that half the White House was in on the program of getting him to concede, for that was the estimate I was repeatedly told. "Sir, I am surprised you're surprised.... In your White House, leaders are telling junior staff this everywhere. I am told this fellow Pat Cipollone [indicating the lawyers behind me as I spoke, not knowing which was Cipollone] has been telling people since November 4, 'Just help us get the President to concede.' And for the last couple of weeks Meadows has been telling staff, 'Help get the President into transition mode.'"

Trump turned to White House General Counsel Pat Cipollone, who began sputtering. "Mr. President, you know how hard I work, you know how many hours I have been putting in..." Both of which were mealy-mouthed, and neither of which was a direct denial, as was obvious to everyone in the room. Trump faced him, his face darkening in anger.

"Sir," I continued, "in 30 minutes I can have two White House staffers here to tell you that those are quotes from Cipollone and Meadows. These guys are lying to you through their teeth. They want you to lose."

Trump turned, knowing I was correct. He indicated one of the other lawyers, said, "Did you know that this is his last day? He has a job starting Monday at a law firm up the street, getting paid 10 times what I can pay him here." He continued wistfully to me, "Pat, can you imagine what I could have gotten done here, if I had not been fighting this for four years?"

Cipollone and the other two lawyers scurried out the back door of the Oval Office. I heard them stay out in the ante room, caucusing. Meanwhile, the President, Sidney, Mike, Alyssa, and myself continued for a while walking through more of the details, reviewing some of what we had said earlier. At some point Allyssa, that quiet but razor-sharp female lawyer assisting Sidney, took over for a few points, and concisely explained aspects of the executive order, always clarifying with great precision whatever needed to be clarified.

After 10 minutes the three lawyers walked back into the room and stood, this time not in the back, but abreast and to the left of we four visitors: Alyssa, myself, Mike, and Sidney, sitting in a half-moon in front of the Resolute desk. Mike continued taking operational questions that arose, while Sidney and Alyssa handled legal questions that arose. The three male lawyers edged closer to the front, then as though as some hidden signal, they all started being bitches.

First was a comment about it not being right to use the National Guard. "The optics are terrible, Mr. President," said one. "It would have to be the DHS." I liked the National Guard idea because we needed to reestablish trust of the American people in the electoral process, and the US institution with the most trust is the one where people dress in military uniforms. Yet the National Guard is local, they are all around us, our colleagues at work, our "Citizen Soldiers".

Perhaps in a sign of flexibility, Flynn and Sidney allowed as how one could use the DHS instead of the National Guard.

At some point Cipollone objected, "Never in American history has there been this kind of a challenge to an election!"

Flynn responded, "Never in American history has there been a situation like this, with counting being shut down for hours, foreigners connecting to our equipment..."

"The press would tear you apart," predicted Pat Cipollone at one turn in the conversation. Sidney said what Mike and I were both thinking: *The press is going to tear him apart? Really? What are they doing now?*

"He does not have the authority to do this!" Cipollone eventually thundered.

Sidney rejoined, "Of course he does," citing EO 13848 (and something else signed by Obama). "Without question he has the authority." Alyssa whipped out EO 13848 again and showed the relevant language that we had covered.

Trump looked at Cipollone with an expression that said, *You never even brought this to my attention, Pat.* He said to Cipollone, "You know Pat, at least they want to fight for me. You don't even fight for me. You just tell me everything I can't do."

By this point Cipollone was getting hot under the collar. Raising his voice to the President, he said, "Hey if you want to do this you don't need my permission. You don't even need a pen or a piece of paper. You can just say, 'I hire Sidney Powell as White House Special Counsel,' and it's done." But then he went on with more objections to everything he was hearing, all of which continued to sound stretched. Even frivolous.

After half-a-dozen such frivolous objections from the White House General Counsel, Mike, Sidney, and I looked at each other dumbstruck. Mike grew calm, silent, his brow knit in bafflement. Finally, I calmly announced to the room: "This is the most surreal conversation I have ever experienced."

Around that time Alyssa spoke up on a legal point: President Trump clearly had grounds to find that those 6 counties had enough peculiarities in their election, that by his powers under those EO's, he was sending in federal teams to recount the ballots in those counties. It was a defensible, reasonable action to take (which she said in legalese). What happened after that would be determined by what was found.

But now the three male lawyers on their feet began speaking to her rudely. They challenged her, asking something like, "You're not even a lawyer!"

She replied, "I *am* a lawyer. I work for Sidney, and-" they cut her off, snorting derisively.

Flynn sprung to his feet with a grace and ease that surprised me, a surfer popping to his feet on a board to catch a wave. He turned to face the three lawyers standing over and barking at Alyssa. In a measured tone he asked of the three lawyers, "Let's get something clear. What do you think happened on November 3? Do you think was a fair election? Nothing unusual about it in your eyes?"

The three lawyers looked down, stuck their toes in the dirt, glanced at each other out of the corners of their eyes, and would not give an answer.

President Trump looked directly at me and said gently, "You know Pat, all my life I've had the best lawyers. People call me from all over the world, 'What lawyer should I use on this? What lawyer should I use on that?' But here.... You know, the other side breaks every rule in the book, nothing ever happens to them, but me? All I have are lawyers who tell me 'You can't do this, you can't do that...' Do you see what I have been working with for four years? Can you imagine what I could have gotten done..." He broke off, then turned to Cipollone, asked "Where's my Durham report? Where's ...." and started rattling off his legal disappointments.

Standing there next to his two colleagues, Cipollone started shouting back at Flynn, still on his feet, *and at the President*. Still shouting, he stepped rudely towards us, standing over (and inappropriately close to) Alyssa from behind. Before I knew it I was on my feet, shoulder-to-shoulder with Flynn, back to the President, with a mental trigger set that if Cipollone moved another inch towards Flynn, Alyssa, or me I was going to bury my knuckles in his throat.

President Trump said, "Hey hey hey!" We all turned. With both hands waiving at us to calm down, and a quarter-smile of disbelief on his face, he said, "Heeey calm down...." Cipollone turned to storm out the door again, his two butt-boys in tow. Before he was out Sidney said, "Let him leave. I'll take the job and you'll win." Trump said after him, "Go ahead Pat. Leave. Don't come back as far as I am concerned." As the door shut, Trump said softly, "Ahhh, I don't mean that. You know, Pat's a friend, and..." his voice trailed off.

I winced at the dawning of my understanding.

I took another shot at it with the President. "Again Sir, I know that Rudy is a friend of yours, he's wonderful. He's America's Mayor. I love Rudy, I don't want to embarrass him. But you should see how what Mike and Sidney have got going. It is so organized, so well-planned-" Again he cut me off, saying, "No no, it's got to be Rudy..." On the inside I slumped.

There was a third round where the lawyers came back in to interject themselves into what the rest of us were talking about. A third round of frivolous push-back, but this time it was President Trump who got ticked off) at the push-back from his own people, the searching for things they could oppose. Again he muttered something weary to me along the lines of, *Can you imagine what I would have accomplish these four years if I had not had to put up with this?*

Finally, at some point President Trump asked why such-and-such a course of action Sidney was proposing had not been explored, the lawyers responded, "Well we're not the campaign lawyers." It was painfully obvious that Cipollone was being purely obstructionist, coming from a place of, *How do I stop this?*

Trump sighed, and wearily said to Cipollone, "You know Pat? A few minutes ago you said that I can make it happen just by *saying* it. Well.... OK. I have decided, now I'm saying it. 'Sidney Powell is hereby appointed as White House Special Counsel'. There, that's it."

"She needs a clearance!" interjected one of the other lawyers. "It'll take months to get her a clearance!"

Even I knew how frivolous that objection was, but Flynn spoke up first. "Mr. President," Flynn said, "you can do the same thing with a clearance. You can grant any clearance you want, on the spot, verbally."

Sadly and defiantly, President Trump looked at his three lawyers and said, "I grant Sidney Powell a Top Secret security clearance."

Again they stormed out of the room. Again the conversation continued among the President, Sidney, Mike, Alyssa, and myself. That is when I had an emotional reaction different than I had expected. There was a moment where I saw him for what he was: a 74 year old man, tired, knowing he was being cheated out of his re-election, maybe defeated, ruing his errors, dwelling on what might have been. I wanted to walk behind his desk, put my arm around him, tell him: *Yes, I do understand what you have been facing. I don't know how you did it.*

Eventually President Trump said that we would all meet in 30 minutes in the living quarters, in the "Yellow Oval". In the meantime, Rudy was coming in and we had to find a way to make things work between Rudy and Sidney. As we parted he said, "You know, in 200 years there probably has not been a meeting in this room like what just happened...". As he was leaving he brushed past me, stopped, and speaking low and quiet, said something quite kind and meaningful, showing me that he knew a lot more about me than I had guessed.

A few minutes later Sidney, Mike, Alyssa, and I were in the Cabinet Room, waiting for Rudy. It was dark, and we had to find a couple lights to turn on. Mike and I were intent on making sure the meeting went well between Sidney and Rudy, so everyone could work happily together.

After 10 minutes Rudy came in, tying his tie, and said in not too gruff a manner, but with perhaps the gruffness of a man disturbed from his evening meal, "You know Sidney, if we are going to work together you have to share information." I did not take his tone as being too aggressive, but one of trying to turn over a new leaf in a relationship, perhaps.

Sidney told him, "I share *everything*, Rudy. You don't read your emails, you don't read your texts."

"That's not true Sidney! I just need you to stop keeping me in the dark-"

"Rudy I don't keep you in the dark! You-"

"Sidney you have to stop keeping everything to yourself! I cannot work with you if you don't share!"

Within moments the conversation had spiraled out of control. After a minute of squabbling I tried to interject something helpful. "Mr. Mayor, it *is* true that since I arrived, everything we brought Sidney, she always said, 'Get this to Rudy right away.' It's true. Absolutely everything we turned up, she told us to share with you. She never asked us to keep you in the dark about anything." But it went poorly.

Fuming, we all went up to the living quarters of the White House.

The President was there, waiting, and after we walked in the three lawyers joined again. Meadows entered as well. A waiter brought out a bowl of small, bottle-cap sized Swedish meatballs, with share plates. Trump motioned for them to be placed at a small table so that everyone could indulge, but the table was in front of me, for which I was grateful. I actually keep vegetarian from time to time, especially when I travel, but how often does one sit with a President serving his grandmother's meatballs? And they were *good*. For the rest of the meeting there were two and only two people eating meatballs: myself, scarfing them down like popcorn, and occasionally the President, who would get up, walk over to me, and refill a small share plate. Nobody else had any.

The meeting continued for a couple hours in those quarters. No substantial new ground was covered: we walked through the reasoning we had gone through in the Oval Office, and the plan. President Trump was decisively onboard, and none of the other parties pushed back. Instead, they glumly asked questions about how such-and-such was to be done, and Mike or Sidney explained. Finally, around 12:15 AM, we all began fading, and wrapped up. We walked outside in the hall, waiting, until the President came out to say goodbye. We each had a moment with him. But we were all exhausted, I think, and glad that the meeting was over.

At no point in the evening was there mention of martial law or Insurrection Act. All claims to the contrary are lies, propagated (I imagine) by Pat Cipollone, who (according to multiple sources) leaks to Maggie Haberman of the NYT. Cursory review of Haberman's writings on the White House, which never fail to give stroke to Cipollone, would support that claim.

Minutes later Alyssa, Sidney, Mike, and I were walking on the sidewalk in front of the White House, light snow still falling in the dark. We saw Meadows and Rudy leave together and walked away to the west. The four of us strode east, elated: with Sidney ensconced as White House Special Counsel, and Mike providing organizational skills and his vast expertise of matters DC, we were in good standing: at that moment we all felt the chance of success high. As we walked home in the snow we confided in each other, *You know, for me this is not really about Trump, but we cannot let a rigged election stand. If we do, it could mean civil war, or a Chinese take-over of our country. All we need is to follow this plan, exposing what happened in those six counties by checking the ballots. If there is nothing amiss, then Trump gets in his helicopter and leaves, and there's no civil war. But if we find chicanery, it will give an opportunity to blow this scheme up for the whole nation. Who knows how much fraud there is going to turn out to be in US elections? I think 'a lot,' what do you think?* Around and around we went, excited for our success in the meeting. After a few blocks our forgotten SUV found us in the flurries, and he drove us the rest of the way to the hotel. I had my first good night's sleep in weeks.

The next day, Saturday, Sidney called Meadows and said, "Well now that I'm White House Special Counsel, I am going to need an office over there."

Meadows told her, "Yeah we're looking into that, we don't have anything immediately, but we are going to soon..."

"Then I will need a White House ID, so I can come and go," replied Sidney.

"Yeah well we are working on that too, there might be a problem with that, we'll see what it is going to take ..." said Meadows.

We all had a terrible sinking feeling, and by Monday or Tuesday, we learned that Sidney's "White House Special Counsel" position was not happening. The plan we had discussed extensively in the White House, the one that got an answer before Christmas (and depending upon the evidence, either permitted a peaceful transition of power, or justified federal involvement that would get to the bottom of the mischief), *that* plan.... had been called off.

Instead, Rudy was going to continue his slog through the courts and the hearings in the states....

Chapter 7: The Christmas Doldrums (December 23 – January 6 noon)

Flynn and Sidney left DC to their own worlds for Christmas, but I was staying around in DC. Before Mike left we had a conversation. I use this opportunity to share a bit about Gneral Mike Flynn.

I knew from people who had worked in the field what Flynn had done to make himself an enemy of the Swamp. When Flynn arrived in Iraq, materials gained in raids were being bundled up in bags, shipped back to Virginia to be "exploited" and analyzed and, weeks later, useful information would be sent back to the troops on the front lines. Flynn sees the world like an entrepreneur, and set about to redesign the process, so that exploitation and analysis was done on-base in Iraq, and the loop condensed into 18 hours: that way, the next night when people went out raiding, they already had the benefit of insights gained from the previous night's work. Eventually the loop was so tightened that a raid early in the evening in one location was generating materials that were studied through the night, and informing raids that were being conducted at dawn.

People I knew and trusted always told me that Flynn had his admirers, but he had detractors as well, primarily those comfortable with the old approach, disgruntled at the way Flynn was shaking things up and bringing modern ideas into the Intelligence Community's way of doing things. As his career progressed Flynn's divisiveness to the Establishment became legendary, but in my experience, men and women I knew who seemed like bright, chipper, mission-oriented federal employees spoke well of Flynn, and the Mediocrities were the ones who seemed to hate him.

But being with Mike Flynn all those weeks, I learned things about him that were new to me. For example, Mike, 61, was a lifelong Democrat, in an Irish Catholic south-of-Boston north-of Providence Jack Kennedy kind of way (not in a modern Lefty, "Let's shred the Constitution!" kind of way). He is a deep reader of the Constitution, and is one of the few people I know (besides myself) who in conversation cites *The Federalist Papers* by number. When discussing America's modern wars, he sounded almost Chomskyan, telling me that the wars in Afghanistan and Iraq should have ended 15 years ago, but so many hundreds of billions and (eventually) trillions of dollars got flowing to the firms that supported the wars, and those firms had grown so fat and hired so many lobbyists, that they fought in DC to keep the wars going so that the spigot would stay turned on. We joked that the war was, "just another Washington, DC self-licking ice cream cone."

In other words, "capture". As happens from time to time, I meet one from a different background who has come to recognize the issue that underlies so many of our problems as a nation. That problem is that powerful elites have captured the decision-making cycles of our government and turned it towards their private ends. The fact that from our different backgrounds and different lifetimes of experience we had arrived at the same fundamental analysis of what is wrong with our country, told me that I my new trail-buddy was the right guy.

Again, before Mike left for Christmas, we had more conversations of form, "General, what the fuck are we doing here?"

I was to be alone in DC over Christmas, but the day before Christmas I got a call from someone in Trump-orbit. The caller told me that I should get down to Florida, to somewhere near Mar-o-Lago, and it was being arranged that I could have another short meeting with Trump, maybe as little as 10 minutes. Because I was by then thoroughly convinced that Trump was not listening to sound people and was missing the Big Picture, I seized the invitation, and went from DC to Florida to a hotel a few miles away from Mar-a-Lago. I checked in, and awaited contact.

Soon I received a call from a well-known person who is publicly associated with Trump, although I do not know how tight they actually are. With him on the call was a colleague of his, and they told me to get over to Mar-a-Lago and ask for "Eileen" (name changed to protect the innocent). I asked for her last name, and was told, "Just get there and ask for Eileen." I asked for Eileen's position, or even what area she worked in. I was told, "Just get to Mar-a-Lago as soon as you can and ask for Eileen." I replied that I really do not like working that way, that I wanted to know more before I went. Again the reply was adamantly, "Get over to Mar-a-Lago, go to the gate, and ask for Eileen. It has all been arranged."

With trepidation I got dressed in my best yoga clothes (my others having been sent out for a rare cleaning) to set out for Mar-a-Lago. I called an Uber, and the ride was a tinny, beat-up Toyota Corolla of some years' vintage.

When I arrived at the gates of Mar-a-Lago I sent the Corolla on its way. I approached the Secret Service detail and told them that I was there to see, "Eileen". The federal agents all looked at each other and shrugged. "Eileen who?" They asked. "I don't know," I told them, "I was just told to ask for Eileen." They again looked at each other with a raised eye. "OK, but Eileen who?" I replied, "I am to have some kind of short meeting with the President, and I was called and told to get here and ask for 'Eileen'." Again, they said, "Well who is Eileen?" Again I had to tell them I did not know. The conversation spiraled downhill from there, through no fault of the Secret Service agents. I perhaps did not help the situation when, noticing that one of the female agents had a light Chinese accent, I began rapping with her in Mandarin in an attempt to calm the situation and establish some rapport. We spoke for a few minutes but it did not calm the other agents. Around that time I began to think it would be best to disengage and get away, and try to work things out by telephone, but the agents did not seem to like that idea.

Eventually the supervising agent came over. He was one of those fellows whom one meets and knows immediately he is not a guy with whom to screw in any way. Still proper but with a fair bit of aggression, he said, "Back up. Start again. We want to know your story. Who are you and what are you doing here?"

Not knowing where to start, I began this way: "20 years ago I started a company called Overstock.com, my name is -." He interrupted with a snort, "Yeah right you're Patrick Byrne." Suddenly I got it: the tiny Corolla, my clothes, the Chinese.... I showed my license again, and this time it all clicked. And it clicked for me, too, how the activities of Flynn, Sidney and I were drawing attention. I was not fully appreciating until then how much attention there was on what we were doing, but it made sense.

In any case, the agents were cordial, nodded to me, and several said, "Thanks for what you are doing," as they permitted me to walk off the property, cross a bridge, and get another Uber.

I hung around an few additional days, waiting for things to be cleared up. They never were. But over those days, I was on the periphery of the Mar-a-Largo crowd and the Republican Pooh-Bah families that were down together for the holidays occupying most of the surrounding hotels. Swimming as I was on the periphery of Republican Party bigwigs and its movers-and-shakers, I got a sense for the *gestalt* of it all. There were some terrific young people, intellectuals who could have deep conversations about ideas as well as events. There was a woman of my age or older, a retired executive from a Fortune 50 company, who was exceedingly strong, capable, and intelligent. Then as far as I could tell, most of the rest were riff-raff. Rich riff-raff, no doubt: shiny-car riff-raff, loud and obnoxious riff-raff, self-centered riff-raff, dilettantes and *poseurs* and grifters of one variety or another, with Plastic Fantastic wives and husbands and doily children whining publicly about whatever subject or thing they felt most deprived. For the most part, not my crowd.

What I did not see were believers, people who had vision.... or a plan.

The day before New Year's Eve I got a call from Our Man in Georgia. We already knew that in Fulton County (in which Atlanta is seated) there was a County Election operation running out of what was called, "the English Street warehouse". An Antifa-looking woman accepted some cash to infiltrate the warehouse, take photos, and seize blank ballots from different stacks. The woman who took these photos snagged blank ballots from different piles.

Our Man in Georgia and I knew that those ballots could be tested forensically.

I lined up two federally-certified forensic document examiners (old-timers in the field) who were willing to work New Year's Day, and got to Georgia on New Year's Eve.

In Georgia, I stayed at the home of some people who were involved in this effort. That is when I first met Jovan Pulitzer (though there had been communication for weeks between my cyber-colleagues and Jovan). Also present was a senior corporate security expert, the man who had found the situation in a counting operation in Savannah, Georgia: a tabulating machine turned out to have a wireless card in it, on the wall there was a Smart Thermostat, and that thermostat had connected wirelessly to the counting machine. Further research had confirmed that someone from China Telecom had come through the Internet onto the Smart Thermostat in order to connect to the machine. The senior cybersecurity expert spent the rest of the evening telling us about the shocking vulnerabilities in the election machines, their tendency to run on Operating System software that was 10-15 years old, and in general, how the technology was Swiss Cheese. We sat up past midnight, with him explaining this to us.

At 3 AM on New Year's Day I received a text from General Flynn. He was still up working as well. He sent me links flashing around social media. Down in Mar-a-Lago, Rudy and others from the entourage had rung in the New Year with a bang. Circulating through social media were photos of Rudy, Don Jr., and Kimberly Gilfoyle drinking champagne, dancing, and Partying Like It's 1999, all to the musical stylings of Vanilla Ice.

Mar-a-Lago was a freak show of D-listers

Again, Flynn and I shared a moment of exasperated silence.

On New Year's Day I was in the laboratory of the federally certified forensic document examiner and a colleague of his colleague who had driven through the night to be there. They were professional, quiet, and I left them to their work. After an hour they reported: two of the ballots were printed in one print shop, the other was printed in a different shop using different paper, different ink, and a different printing method. It being unlikely the county had ordered ballots from two different print shops, this indicated that at least one of those ballots was counterfeit.

Our Man in Georgia had Atlanta warehouse under observation, bums with telephoto lenses filming. The Georgia Senate demanded to inspect the contents of the English Street warehouse. Hours later, rented Enterprise vans pulled up to the warehouse, and loaded pallets of ballots.

Armed Trafficking of Ballots from election Prep Center to Sheriff Jackson's Office

The next day, a shredding company in a neighboring county got a phone call to pick up an assignment to shred. The truck pulled up and loaded approximately 3,000 pounds of ballots. The person who made the call identified himself as being with "Dominion Moving", but when he paid for the shredding he paid with a credit card from "Dominion Voting Systems". The shredding truck pulled away. Through a mechanism I will not disclose, that shredding truck was intercepted, its work stopped, and ultimately, 10,000 pounds of shredded material was dumped out on the floor of a local police station, so there would be a chain-of-evidence. Roughly 3,000 pounds of the shredded material was the ballots (the other 7,000 was from prior customers). The shredding that had been order by the Dominion Voting employee had not been normal shredding (turning pages into long strips); it had not been special shredding (turning pages into confetti); it had been the super-duper military-grade shredding, where the ballots had been shredded then crushed down to spitballs.

An Atlanta DHS agent arrived and took command. A discovery was made: some of the shredded ballots had not been *completely* shredded. In fact, a few had stuck to the walls of the bin, and were whole. Also found, I was told, were receipts and shipping labels from the boxes that held the ballots: these receipts and shipping labels were from a Chinese print shop in the south of China. The DHS agent acquired all of these (and that particular agent is one with an expertise in matters Chinese, I am told).

Call that moment, "T = 0". Based on the continuous reports I was receiving from Atlanta, here is how the next two days unfolded:

- T + 6 hours: Rudy Giuliani was informed of what was going on;
- T + 12 hours: Mark Meadows was informed of what was going on
- T + 18 hours: FBI arrived on the scene to take over. DHS resisted.
- T + 24 hours: I received a message that the DHS agent in question was uncomfortable with the political pressure he was receiving. If I understood correctly, he was saying that Meadows himself (Chief of Staff of the White House) had called him and told him to back off the investigation. It was not clear to me whether I was receiving the message just as a bystander, or the DHS agent was causing that mes-

sage to come to me in the incorrect hope I could do something about it (e.g., get it to the President).

- T + 36 hours: The FBI took control of the operation. They instructed the shredding company to come back, pick up the 10,000 pounds of material, complete the shredding, then continue with their normal procedures. That meant the shredded material was mixed with water and acid, melted, then reconstituted as recycled paper.

Various aspects of the story I told above are documented in photos and film.

Meanwhile, I had returned to DC. I was still trying to get another 10 minutes with Trump. I wanted to remind him again that if he waited then tried the plan that we had been proposing, it would be sore loser-ism. But we still had a few days left, and if he pulled the trigger, we could have an answer regarding those Problematic 6 counties. We could have it done before January 6, so that the Senate might make an informed choice, or buy us an extra week to do more work, or or or...

At this point I will insert one important sub-story. In those days of swimming around with people who were in various proximities to the President, I was told something by someone in Trump's inner circle: Melania had recently been warned by a government official that if Donald Trump served another term, he would be JFK'ed. It may have been said by someone in the Secret Service itself, in a "We will not be able to protect him" sense. The threat included another family member as well, per the telling. I find it hard to believe that anyone in the Secret Service itself would say that, but the source of the information to me had been otherwise blemishless, and the claim was that whoever (perhaps Secret Service, perhaps someone else) had said this to Melania, it was someone from whom such a claim would be taken seriously. Melania was begging Donald not to fight, and simply to concede and leave Washington with his family.

In the days before the Georgia runoff election on January 5, Marc Elias won a filing *against* purging a couple hundred thousand names from voter polls before the runoff. The judge who ruled in his favor (on the left) is the sister of Stacey Abrams.

Mike Flynn and I were together again in DC, watching the approaching January 6 date with frustration. I had done several interviews and even a public speech or two where I had insisted that, "We do not go violent, we are better than the other guys, if we go violent, we lose." I thought it too obvious to dwell on, but I said it in numerous public addresses and interviews.

On the morning of January 5, a meeting was had by myself and a few of our scientists and dolphin-speakers, and a variety of senators and delegates of senators, a delegate of VP Mike Pence, and delegates of other interested parties. The scientists laid out the case simply and clearly. They answered questions for a couple hours, and after those couple hours, it was clear no one doubted what we were telling them: that a sophisticated operation had rigged the presidential election. The delegate from VP Pence went directly back from our meeting to brief the VP, I was told.

I am told that Pence heard the briefing, agreed with its implications, and decided on a course of action: when he stood before the Senate the next day, January 6, he was going to call for a 7 day suspension, so that the individual state legislatures could look into whatever they wanted to look into, even perform quick investigations, then re-vote their electoral votes. Both on the day in question and days later, this fact was confirmed to me: at 3:30 PM on January 5, Pence was solidly there.

I had been invited to speak on the morning of January 6, on the South Lawn, by the Women for Trump who had organized the rally. I prepared a talk to hit two points: how our system of consent of the governed relies on elections that are free, fair, and transparent (which our November election was not). Secondly, we do not use violence.

I was torn between two ways of making the point about non-violence:

1. Telling a Jerry Garcia and the Grateful Dead story regarding non-violence (which I have written up on Deep Capture as: Jerry Garcia on Confrontation & "The Main Asshole").
2. Telling a story I told about Moldova. I had been there a few years earlier, and a barman had told me of the 2009 election. Election fraud had caused a pro-Putin man to be elected, but the people knew of the fraud and had risen up in protests. Putin had sent hundreds of men to drift into the capital of Chisinau, and they had a mission: every time there was a protest, these Putin-guys had infiltrated it with a goal of turning it violent, getting them not just to protest *in front of* government buildings, but to charge them, break windows, occupy them. The Moldovans had been too smart for the trick: they knew Putin understood that both sides were playing for an audience, the middle class of Moldova, and if the protesters were able to be provoked into actually storming government buildings it would turn off the middle class and they would lose the support of the masses. The Moldovans had stayed disciplined, refused to let themselves be led astray like that... and eventually the government had succumbed, a new, fair election was held, and the Putin crony lost. I wrote that story up as well: "A Message to Militias Across America Regarding the Goon-Left and *Agents Provocateurs* (Not the Lingerie)".

I was not sure which story I would use on the White House lawn. On the 5th, I decided that the crowd might not know who Jerry Garcia was, so I decided to write that story up online and tweet it out a couple times to the throngs who were arriving in DC, and rehearsed a concise explanation of the Moldova story to use on the morning of January 6 when I spoke.

Mike Flynn was going to be speaking too, we were informed. Mike and I spoke about what we were going to say, what the crowd needed to hear. We recognized it as a unique historical opportunity: we would have perhaps 30 minutes to explain to the world the irregularities that had disrupted the election, and most likely had changed its outcome. We prepared to meet that challenge. We understood that some of the people with whom we had been working, the cyber-ninjas and scientists and such, were also preparing concise explanations, but the choice of who among them was going to be speaking was being handled by the organizers.

Mike and I thought that the morning of January 6 was going to run like this: there would be speeches on the South Lawn of the White House. He would give a talk as "The People's General" setting the moment in its historical context. I would talk about the fundamental significance of elections that were free, fair, and transparent, and then tell my Moldova story. Then we would switch to 2-3 of these cyber-ninjas and scientists, who would each talk for 5-10 minutes, explaining the irregularities that should trouble the conscience of citizens. I knew from experience that any one of them could speak for 5-10 minutes and cause any thinking person to have grave doubts about the November 2020 election, but I figured that with three of them speaking, 80% of the viewers around the world would understand why Election 2020 results had to be seriously discounted.

I got a call from one of the scientists I expected to speak. He was letting me know he could not come to DC because he his speaking slot had been cancelled. I was perplexed, because this scientist was soft-spoken, professorial, and convincing. I wondered whom they had found to do a better job than he of convincing millions of viewers that they should be skeptical of what happened during the week of November 3.

On the morning of the 6th, Flynn, myself and some of the cyber-ninjas met to discuss the previous day's election run-off in Georgia. One of the ninjas had already extracted and mapped the data, and we saw that the Goons were not even trying to hide it (see the 11:08 PM event below):

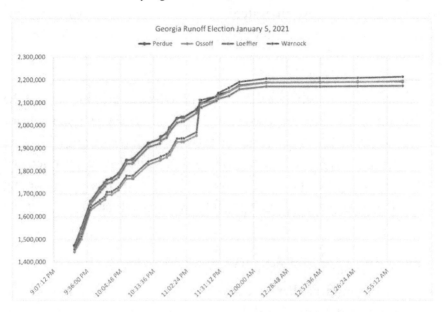

Again, voters had gone to bed thinking two candidates were well ahead, and woke up to two swings of virtually-identical sizes that delivered the races to their opponents:

Candidate	Jan. 5 10:51PM	Jan. 6 8:41AM	Diff
Perdue	1,990,928	2,192,347	201,419
Ossoff	1,871,066	2,208,717	337,651
Diff	119,862	(16,370)	136,232

Candidate	Jan. 5 10:51PM	Jan. 6 8:41AM	Diff
Loeffler	1,999,338	2,173,866	174,528
Warnock	1,929,323	2,227,296	297,973
Diff	70,015	(53,430)	123,445

The Georgia Overnight Vote Swing

"They're laughing at us," Flynn said, correctly. "They're doing it openly to say, 'We have all the instruments of power, the courts, the press, the Establishment, we are just going to do this in front of your faces.' They know we know, they know we are watching, and they do it openly because the damn system is so corrupt they think there's nothing we can do. They're just laughing at us."

Flynn, myself, and about a dozen with us walked to the south side of the White House. We were surprised that no arrangements had been made for us as speakers, and we had to fight our way through the throngs. We were given speakers' badges, seated in a special section up front... then learned that our speaking slots had been cancelled. We were perplexed, wondering whom they could get that would possibly explain the situation as well as we could.

Meanwhile, up at the White House.... I later learned from proverbial "White House insiders" that on Tuesday afternoon, January 5, at *3:30* PM, Pence had indeed, "been there". He had been ready to stand up in front of the Senate on January 6 and call for a 7 day recess, to let the states consider all the information that had come in (and could be generated) about election irregularities, then re-commit their electoral votes. And he stayed that way all the way until Tuesday at *6:30* PM. At that point, a gentleman named Marc Short (Chief of Staff of VP Pence) had talked Pence out of it.

Marc Short is a Legislative Affairs Swamp Creature: whatever he whispered in Pence's ear, it was enough to get Pence to flip-flop, back to the position that his position in the Senate was only ministerial, almost ritualistic. Pence informed President Trump on the morning of the 6th that he was not going to do anything heroic. There had been quite a clash within the White House that ranged from the Oval Office to the Living Quarters, but had ended with Pence unmoved: his job was to open the envelopes and read the electoral votes.

That was all going on a few hundred yards away from me, but I did not know it at the time, of course.

The show finally started, and soon Flynn and I sunk into our seats in despair. One Trump child sang "Happy Birthday" to someone. Rudy spoke about Joe Frazier voting. Another lawyer spoke. Don Jr. strode the stage talking about how the Republican brand was now the Trump brand, or the Trump brand was the Republican brand. Flynn and I caught eyes and shared looks of horror: it turned out later we were both asking if the other wanted to leave. It was so bad that one of the organizers had a change of heart and came running over to ask Flynn if he would take the stage: he refused. It went on for what seemed like ages until Trump appeared and spoke, much as he would at any campaign event. In fact, the whole thing was more or less a "I was robbed" pep rally: no real effort was made to explain to the crowd, to the Senators who would begin voting in an hour, to the Americans watching at home, to the world that counts on America to be the leader of free, fair, and transparent elections, what went wrong with the November 2020 election, and why they should believe that Election 2020 had deep irregularities demanding investigation. No significant effort at all.

Instead, it was a pep rally. That's it. If they'd given 10 minutes to each of two different names I'd given them, two scientists who know this issue intimately, history would have been different. I think that 20 minutes would have changed the hearts of a significant number of senators about the need for a week's worth of hearings before the Senate signed off on things.

But it was a Trump "I was robbed" pep rally.

The moment we could make a break from the front, Flynn and I and everyone with us made a dash for the exit. Flynn could barely contain his fury as we shared impressions: this had been the one last chance to explain the situation to the world, and instead Trump had used it as a pep rally. "He just does not get it," we repeated to each other as we stormed through the crowd back towards the hotel. "He does not get that it is not about him. He put on a fucking pep rally. He does not understand that this is not about him," we repeated in despair. In 15 minutes we were back at the hotel, both packing our bags, both nauseous, and did not leave to join the throngs moving towards the Capitol.

Chapter 8: Agitation & Chaos: January 6 (noon) – 20

TOOELE COUNTY SHERIFF'S OFFICE

What happened on the afternoon of January 6 is the worst thing that could happen for the Freedom Movement. Millions descended on DC to rally in support of those standing for the truth: our election was rigged. In the course of the rally, Goons stormed the Capitol.

One woman (an Air Force vet) was shot unnecessarily by police.

The New York Times reported that a policeman was killed, his head bashed in by protester's fire extinguisher. Then that story got wobbly:

> "Media reports have been conflicting — unnamed law enforcement sources initially told outlets Sicknick was bludgeoned in the head by a fire extinguisher, while others speaking on condition of anonymity countered those claims, arguing there was no immediate evidence showing

that Sicknick suffered any blunt force trauma" ("A month after Capitol riot, autopsy results pending in Officer Brian Sicknick death investigation", Fox, February 8 2021).

In Mid-February the *New York Times* retracted: it turns out the officer died from a stroke (while the media milked the Sicknick story for a month, this was known two days after his death):

The Times Corrects the Record on Officer Sicknick's Death, Sort Of

Andrew C. McCarthy · 2/15/2021

A few days ago, the *New York Times* quietly "updated" its report, published over a month earlier, asserting that Capitol Police officer Brian Sicknick had been killed by being struck with a fire extinguisher during the January 6 riot.

© Erin Schaff/Reuters   The hearse carrying the remains of Capitol Police officer Brian Sicknick leave the Capitol in Washington, D.C., February 3, 2021.

'The *Times* Corrects the Record on Officer Sicknick's Death, Sort Of".
Finally, on February 23: "Capitol Police Officer Brian Sicknick's Mother: 'He Wasn't Hit on the Head' on Jan. 6" (*Epoch Times*):

> "The mother of Capitol Police officer Brian Sicknick said her son was not beaten with a fire extinguisher by

a mob on Jan. 6, saying he likely suffered a stroke instead—refuting reports from the New York Times and other outlets claiming otherwise.

"'He wasn't hit on the head, no. We think he had a stroke, but we don't know anything for sure...'"

Mainstream Media sought to increase the public's horror by increasing the body count, including, for example, two police officers who committed suicide in the days after the attack:

AXIOS

2 Capitol Police officers died by suicide days after the Jan. 6 assault on Congress

"2 Capitol Police officers died by suicide days after the Jan. 6 assault on Congress, *Axios*, February 13, 2021

During 2020, Mainstream Media described the actions of Antifa and Black Lives Matter killing 33 police, injuring another 700 police, and burning thousands of businesses as "mostly peaceful protests":

There are two ways to look at what happened on that fateful afternoon at the Capitol. I think they are both true, though which is more true is, at the moment, anyone's guess.

> **The Party Line Explanation**: splinter elements ($\approx$ 400 people) of the millions of protesters stormed the Capitol. Given that this Party Line explanation has been repeated *ad nauseum* by a supine and obedient press, and is currently the object of an impeachment of a man who is no longer an officeholder (go figure), I will not spend time developing this interpretation. But I do not mean to discount it, either.

> **The Alternative Explanation** is more subtle, and runs along the lines of my story about Moldova explained in, "A Message to Militias Across America Regarding the Goon-Left and *Agents Provocateurs* (Not the Lingerie)":

Patrick Byrne

The oligarchy has two wings: Wall Street and the Deep State. I have been hunting both since 2004.

A Message to Militias Across America Regarding the Goon-Left and Agents Provocateurs (Not the Lingerie)

January 17, 2021 · 6 min read

On the morning of January 6 a stranger approached me and told me he was a militia member. He spoke of a concept with which I was unfamiliar, "The 3%", and said it was a reference to the fraction of the population who fought and won our Revolution. The stranger told me there were tens of thousands of them around the county in communications on the dark web, armed and ready. He told me something that blew my mind: they know who I am, and are willing to do whatever I tell them needs to be done. I just need to give the word.

This explanation holds that the events were engineered as part of a psyop to discredit those skeptical of the election result, and to justify a police-state-style crackdown by the Goon-Left on the rest of America. To those not used to thinking in the bank-shot terms of a psyop, that may seem odd, but I wish to remind the reader that the evidence has been in front of us for nearly 9 months, with regard to Black Lives Matter.

A Brief Digression on Black Lives Matter

After publishing this book, I intend to write an essay about the Supreme Court, and then a piece I anticipate titling, "An Analytic Philosopher Takes Black Lives Matter Ideological Purity Test, Scores ≈ 40%". In brief, I will argue, the BLM phrase suffers from semantic overload, and it has to be unpacked into a set of about half-a-dozen assertions, which I will explore individually. I agree with some, I do not with others: like I say, I predict I will score a 40% (maybe a bit higher). My bottom line for the BLM movement is what it is for the Left in general: usually correct about the problems, generally (but not always) incorrect about how to fix the problems.

Yet that my point in bringing them up here is not to debate that issue. I am friendly with three people whom one might call "radical Black Muslim activists" (and yes, it is an interesting and occasionally tempestuous friendship). They are quite "woke": I say I am not woke because I never slept (but I am not sure they buy it).

In any case, when last summer the BLM demonstrations started began getting violent, my friends started telling me of eye-opening rumors in their community. There were agitators showing up at BLM rallies in Black neighborhoods, White people dressed in black and with masks, agitating for violence. Videos emerged documenting precisely what my friends were warning me about, masked and fully covered men slipping through a crowd, going up to a shop window with hammers, smashing the windows, then slipping away (and when there is a crowd of demonstrators, once windows get smashed, the demonstration turns into looting).

Right-wing provocateurs continue to instigate violence at BLM protests and elsewhere

 Kevin Shay May 31, 2020 · 7 min read ✶

Boogaloo Bois and others join both BLM and pro-Trump actions to further goal of societal collapse

This story was updated on Jan. 15, 2021.

Violence at political protests has long been inflamed by provocateurs, including by those who seek to infiltrate the demonstrations and cause violence to make the cause look bad. That happened in the civil rights movement of the 1950s and 1960s, the anti-war demonstrations of the 1960s, and the anti-nuclear protests of the 1980s, among others.

Left-wing journalist Kevin Shay wrote on May 31, 2020: "Right-wing *provocateurs* continue to instigate violence at BLM protests and elsewhere".

Far-right extremists keep showing up at BLM protests. Are they behind the violence?

BY JUDY L. THOMAS

JUNE 16, 2020 12:50 PM , UPDATED JUNE 16, 2020 11:15 PM

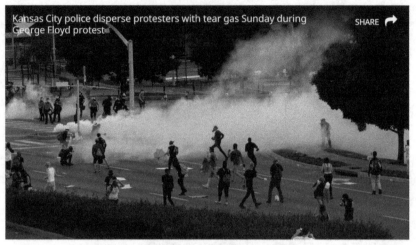

Kansas City police disperse protesters with tear gas Sunday during George Floyd protest

SHARE

Protesters scatter after Kansas Cit police throw tear gas into the crowd Sunday, May 31, 2020, at the George Floyd protest near the Country Club Plaza. BY KYLIE GRAHAM

The meme continued: on June 16, 2020, *Kansas City Star* asked, "Far-right extremists keep showing up at BLM protests. Are they behind the violence?"

As I remember, evidence emerged that confirmed the story of provocateurs infiltrating BLM protests and turning them violent. Some of the evidence was that right-wing people had done it, in order to provoke violence. Some of the evidence pointed at Antifa. But in either case, let me point out that for 9 month the US political discourse has the first time admitted the concept of *provocateur*. It is no longer some arcane concept known only to everyone in the world outside of the USA: *we* now understand that crowds get infiltrated and manipulated.

The Alternative Hypothesis for the January 6 events at the Capitol is that to some degree the events resulted from such provocation. It is a claim that the "insurrection" was, in a way, engineered, in order to benefit people who would benefit politically from it.

What evidence supports this Alternative Explanation, that the ransacking of the Capitol was *invited* by those who would make hay from it politically? Let us review some evidence:

On January 12, an article from the *Independent Sentinel* ("Pelosi-McConnell refused to increase security! Capitol emergency began before Trump finished speaking", January 11), appeared describing a *Washington Post* article from the previous day.

Capitol Police Chief Steven Sund testifies before House lawmakers in July 2019. (Congressional Quarterly/CQ Roll Call/AP)

"The Washington Post reported late Sunday night that the outgoing Capitol Police Chief, Steve Sund, believes his efforts to secure the premises were undermined by a lack of concern from House and Senate security officials who answer directly to Speaker Nancy Pelosi and Senate leader Mitch McConnell."

Then quoting from the *WaPo*:

"Two days before Congress was set to formalize President-elect Joe Biden's victory, Capitol Police Chief Steven

Sund was growing increasingly worried about the size of the pro-Trump crowds expected to stream into Washington in protest.

"To be on the safe side, Sund asked House and Senate security officials for permission to request that the D.C. National Guard be placed on standby in case he needed quick backup.

"But, Sund said Sunday, they turned him down...

"It was the first of six times Sund's request for help was rejected or delayed, he said. Two days later on Wednesday afternoon, his forces already in the midst of crisis, Sund said he pleaded for help five more times as a scene far more dire than he had ever imagined unfolded on the historic Capitol grounds.

Besides the higher-ups preventing the police protecting the Capitol to increase their presence when asked, is there other evidence that suggests the occupation of the Capitol was to some degree *invited*?

In the following clip police can, in fact, be seen *inviting* protesters past the barricades:

Capitol Police Allow Protesters to Reach the Capitol

Capitol Police Allow Protesters to Reach the Capitol

And here, a video clip that shows the police just *letting* the protesters take the Hill:

Cops allow protestors to take Capitol hill | Police department let protesters in

Here police stand aside and let the Capitol be assaulted (while bystanders *beg* them to stop it)

Here some Antifa were caught changing into MAGA clothes just outside the Capitol:

ANTIFA CAUGHT CHANGING INTO MAGA GEAR IN BUSHES AT D.C. CAPITOL

Here are patriots catching on and trying to stop the Antifa/BLM agitators:

Patriot Stopping Antifa From Breaking DC Capitol Building Windows

Here one can see someone inside the Capitol handing weapons to those *outside* the Capitol so they will be able to break their way in:

ANTIFA given weapons from inside capitol building

T *Trump20XX* · Published January 9, 2021 · 48,240 Views

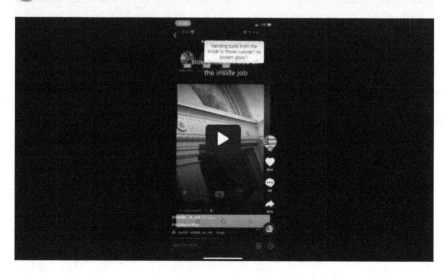

ANTIFA given weapons from inside capitol building

Then in this clip police do... exactly what the title claims:

Capitol police open doors for the protestors. They stand aside and invite them inside

And this one ("Police open the doors of the capital and invite everyone in"):

Police open the doors of the capital and invite everyone in

Liberty · Published January 12, 2021 · 44,991 Views   SUBSCRIB

3 rumbles   EMBED ↗

Rumble — This Video is 1 minute after Ashli has been shot less than 50 feet away. It was taken at the east wing door as the cops unlock the doors.

Police open the doors of the capital and invite everyone in

And this remarkable one (which wins my "Ed Wood Action Sequence Award"):

DC Capital Police Lets Protestors Enter and Storm US Capitol Building

Patriot Prosperity · Published January 7, 2021 · 47,322 Views   SUBSCRIBE 36K   SHARE ⤴

Military Troops from 2nd Cavalry...
Patriot Prosperity

DC Capital Police Allowing Protestor...
Patriot Prosperity

Protestors Storm The Capitol Building
HodgeTwins

DC Police usher MAGA Trump...
Trump20XX

Trump Protestors
STORM Capitol Hill

685 rumbles   EMBED ↗

DC Capital Police Lets Protestors Enter and Storm US Capitol Building

Here is a policeman being "overwhelmed" with invaders. Does anything look staged about this?

DC Capital Police Allowing Protestors To Enter and Storm US Capitol

And here is the famous Q Shaman with eight photojournalists. Anything here looked staged?

Here is a good "synch edit" showing a policeman taking careful aim then shooting an unarmed (female) protester in the throat. She died.

Capitol 2021 Ashli Babbitt sync edit

Interestingly, the identity of the policeman who shot the unarmed female protester in the throat has been closely guarded. There are as yet *unconfirmed* reports that this is he.

In fairness, I wish to emphasize that authorities will not speak on the matter of the shooter's identity, one way or another. If it was indeed Officer Bailey, I should note that it appears he was at the shooting of Congressman Scalise, and was injured there himself. If those facts all prove true, I will note that one could understand why the officer might have been a little quicker on the trigger than he could have been.

In that crowd of protesters in the hallway when the female was shot above, one spots this individual:

TOOELE COUNTY SHERIFF'S OFFICE

His name is John Sullivan and he is a Utah-based Antifa/BLM activist ("Utah Man with a History of Organizing Violent Antifa, BLM Protests, Was Inside the Capitol"). He organized a BLM rally an hour earlier that day, 11 AM, and tweeted about BLM Buses ("Utah Activist John Sullivan Organized Antifa Protest Near US Capitol Before It Was Stormed — Tweeted About BLM Buses in DC on the 6th). This is important because later there were reports of buses escorted to the front of the capitol from which early rioters emerged.

He was arrested for his actions in the Capitol that day, then released without charges once his Lefty political preferences were discovered.

Does that seem odd? Not anymore.

(Photo : Mika Baumeister / Unsplash)

Antifa infiltrated President Donald Trump's supporters of the Save America Rally on their way to the U.S. Capitol yesterday according to surfacing evidence and as lawmakers alleged themselves,

The Mainstream Media was originally allowed to discuss this possibility.

- The *NY Post* published: "Two known Antifa members posed as pro-Trump to infiltrate Capitol riot: sources" (Jan 7).
- "Antifa Infiltrated Trump Supporters In Capitol, Evidence Reveals" (*Christianity Today*, Jan 8).

For further interest, I suggest watching this 21-minute mini-documentary:

EVERYTHING WRONG WITH THE CAPITOL SHOOTING IN 21 MINUTES OR LESS

So was the storming of the Capitol a disgrace? Yes.

Was it also engineered and/or staged? Put me down as, "Undecided". Lol

On the 7th of January, five minutes after the Senate had selected Joseph Biden to be President, DNI John Ratcliffe delivered the homework assignment which had been due for him on December 18. He opened it up with a rather dramatic and unequivocal statement: that the report from the IC community that he then oversaw inadequately reflected China's role in affecting the US election, and notes that an accompanying Ombudsman's report highlights the worst sin of which intelligence analysts can be accused: politicizing the intelligence product. DNI Ratcliffe's letter (which the MSM has already flushed down the Orwellian Memory Hole) is so shocking I am going to quote the first 50% of it:

Ratcliffe - Views on Intelligence Community Election Security Analysis

SUBJECT: Views on Intelligence Community Election Security Analysis

REFERENCE: Intelligence Community Assessment: Foreign Threats to the 2020 U.S. Elections

From my unique vantage point as the individual who consumes all of the U.S. government's most sensitive intelligence on the People's Republic of China, I do not believe the majority view expressed by Intelligence Community (IC) analysts fully and accurately reflects the scope of the Chinese government's efforts to influence the 2020 U.S. federal elections.

The IC's Analytic Ombudsman issued a report, which I will reference several times below, that includes concerning revelations about the politicization of China election influence reporting and of undue pressure being brought to bear on analysts who offered an alternative view based on the intelligence. The Ombudsman's report, which is being transmitted to Congress concurrently with this Intelligence Community Assessment (ICA), also delves into a wider range of election security intelligence issues that I will not focus on here. However, the specific issues outlined below with regard to China reporting are illustrative of broader concerns. It is important for all IC leaders to foster a culture within the Community that encourages dissenting views that are supported by the intelligence. Therefore, I believe it is incumbent upon me in my role as the Director of National Intelligence to lead by example and offer my analytic assessment, alongside the majority and minority views. This letter was prepared in consultation with the Ombudsman to ensure that I am accurately articulating his findings and presenting them in their proper context.

The majority view expressed in this ICA with regard to China's actions to influence the election fall short of the mark for several specific reasons.

The majority view expressed in this ICA with regard to China's actions to influence the election fall short of the mark for several specific reasons.

Analytic Standard B requires the IC to maintain "independence of political considerations." This is particularly important during times when the country is, as the Ombudsman wrote, "in a hyper partisan state." However, the Ombudsman found that:

> "China analysts were hesitant to assess Chinese actions as undue influence or interference. These analysts appeared reluctant to have their analysis on China brought forward because they tend to disagree with the administration's policies, saying in effect, I don't want our intelligence used to support those policies. This behavior would constitute a violation of Analytic Standard B: Independence of Political Considerations (IRTPA Section 1019)."

Furthermore, alternative viewpoints on China's election influence efforts have not been appropriately tolerated, much less encouraged. In fact, the Ombudsman found that:

SUBJECT: Views on Intelligence Community Election Security Analysis

"There were strong efforts to suppress analysis of alternatives (AOA) in the August [National intelligence Council Assessment on foreign election influence], and associated IC products, which is a violation of Tradecraft Standard 4 and IRTPA Section 1017. National Intelligence Council (NIC) officials reported that Central Intelligence Agency (CIA) officials rejected NIC coordination comments and tried to downplay alternative analyses in their own production during the drafting of the NICA."

Additionally, the Ombudsman found that CIA Management took actions "pressuring [analysts] to withdraw their support" from the alternative viewpoint on China "in an attempt to suppress it. This was seen by National Intelligence Officers (NIO) as politicization," and I agree. For example, this ICA gives the false impression that the NIO Cyber is the only analyst who holds the minority view on China. He is not, a fact that the Ombudsman found during his research and interviews with stakeholders. Placing the NIO Cyber on a metaphorical island by attaching his name alone to the minority view is a testament to both his courage and to the effectiveness of the institutional pressures that have been brought to bear on others who agree with him.

DNI Ratcliffe claimed that he had not wanted to deliver the report any earlier because it would have "politicized" the Constitutional process of selecting the next president that was then occurring. He was another Republican concerned about "optics". Call me "crazy", but myself, I believe the correct analysis would have been, "I should deliver this report on time so that the Constitutionally-stipulated process for selecting the next President is fully informed, and if that includes that the election involved foreign interference, particularly from China, I have an obligation to make sure that is known to those involved in that process."

Moving on....

Sidney had left before January 6, but after the events of January 6, Mike Flynn, the cyber-ninjas, dolphin-speakers, and I had our last talks, said our goodbyes.

On the evening of January 6, I received a 10:30 PM phone call telling me that Rudy Giuliani requested my presence at his hotel. The intermediary said, "We are about ready to hang up our gloves on this, but we want to talk to you about your ideas." I walked over to Rudy's hotel. When I got there, I found 8 people in a suite. Rudy was there, along with the Commish, Mediocrity, a smart lawyer, and a handful of others. I sat down in front of Rudy and they repeated: they were ready to stop, but wanted to see if I had any ideas.

As I began reply Rudy began checking his phones, fumbling with two or three of them, reading texts, etc. For the first time I did what I should have done two months earlier: I stopped talking. He said, "No no, go ahead." I stayed silent and stared at him. He said, "I can't turn these off, I might get a call from the President."

"Then please give them to" Mediocrity, I said surprising myself at my rudeness. Then to Mediocrity: "Keep an eye on them and let Mayor Giuliani know if the President calls."

Rudy put his phones down and slid them to Mediocrity. As I began again to speak, Mediocrity began having a side conversation, and again I folded my hands, stared at Mediocrity. I wondered if it ever occurred to them that calling someone at 10:30 PM to come provide assistance, then gabbing in front of them and checking texts, was in any way rude? I think not. In any case, Mediocrity cut off the side conversation and faced me quietly. Everyone else in the room went quiet as well, and looked at me.

In two months of dealing with that group, it was the first moment that they conducted themselves in a manner that businesspeople (or even, "normal adults") conduct themselves. I realized that for the first time I had Rudy's full attention, and I could see it was the first time he was the Rudy Giuliani I remember from 30 years ago, in command, focused, ready to take on the Mob. The silence stretched on as I thought, then said:

> "These machines were sold to the public with a promise: as a fail-safe there would always be paper ballots to use as a backup. If there was ever a time, now is the time. The FBI and CISA have opined that our election came under foreign attack. We provided evidence of that as well. President Trump should find that there has been foreign interference, and on that basis send a federal force of US Marshalls, or National Guard, or DHS, or FBI, to examine paper ballots in the problematic six counties, and count them on livestream TV. If there are no gross irregularities, he should concede. But if he finds discrepancies of hundreds of thousands of ballots, as we think he may, he then

has choices. He can recount the six states, or order the federal force to rerun the election in those 6 states. He might even be able to have it all done by January 20."

There was silence. After a few seconds the Commish stirred to speak. I turned to face him as he slid his hand away from his mouth and stroked his chin. He nodded slowly, and grunted, "Yeah. Makes sense." Mediocrity lit up, and the new lawyer on the scene, on my left, spoke up and began exploring the advantages of it aloud. Rudy chimed in, and within minutes they were working it out: it was narrow so it was not too objectionable, it generated an answer, and depending upon the outcome, it gave a route not only to Trump but to answering a question that has hung over US for decades: how much election fraud is there? I stayed another 30 minutes as they bounced the idea around with a spark of excitement growing. Finally they said they would be working on details and maybe even calling the President, and I took that as my cue to leave. I said goodbye to them, and put my coat on.

As I turned to leave the Mayor came and shook my hand. Then he tapped my chest with his finger and said quietly, regretfully: "If *only* we had another month."

Truly. I had watched two months slide by Mayor Giuliani and his team while they dispayed no organization or progress. Watching them try to get anything done *was* like watching half-a-dozen monkeys trying to fuck a football. But now, "If only we had another month." They could have had another *decade* and it would not have made a difference. They were the wrong people. Rudy, because he should not be handling complex litigation, he certainly should not be handling complex litigation regarding cyber, and because he'd rather spend his days doing podcasts. A former fed who was so Mediocre we all came to suspect was sent as an agent of disruption, and others focused on a pot of cash that (at last report) was $300 million and growing.

I walked the snow-covered midnight streets of Washington DC back to my hotel and finished packing for my departure.

Over the next couple of days we all drifted away, back to our normal lives. On the 8th, I checked out, experiencing yet again at the discontent I feel most times I have affairs that in DC. Discontent with people whose sense of accomplishment is so skewed (bureaucrats measure their output in a paradigm of thwarting other factions, not in anything that normal people would count as "accomplishment"), at the cost to the country of DC, at the staggering wealth that has accumulated there (cf., "DC Suburbs Now Contain 7 Of America's 10 Richest Counties," *Slate*, September 2012). It has become *Hunger Games* without the archery. But there were people I had gotten to know over the previous several months, had grown to like and respect, and I had opportunity to visit with most of them individually and say goodbye.

I returned to my home in Utah Saturday the 9th feeling under the weather, but intent on writing the story you have been reading. By on the morning of Monday, January 11, I tested positive for Covid, as I had come to suspect. I took it easy for a few days with a fever of 101, still brushing it off, telling myself that, "On a Flu Scale of 1-10, this is a 2. They shut down the world for this?" I woke Thursday, January 14, feeling almost fine, with a temperature back under 100. I thought I was through it. But by afternoon I began feeling ill again, and within an hour my temperature was 105.4. I barely made it to a hospital, and when I did they put me on monoclonal antibodies due to risk factors too numerous and depressing to list. Dealing with that and the Covid Fog that followed cost me 10 days.

On January 20, the day that Biden was sworn in as President, I got phone calls from two different Trump White House staffers. They wanted to tell me a story before they left Washington for the last time. The stories they told me matched in detail. I will relate it here.

On January 18, some loyal staffers had been visiting with Trump in his office for what was supposed to be a 10 minute goodbye. But the discussion had turned to the election, and before long Trump was rehashing the decisions he had made, wondering if he had made mistakes. The subject turned to Sidney, Mike, and me, and the plan we had brought the White House. Trump walked through it with these staffers for a few minutes, I was told, before it all clicked for him. "That's it?" He asked angrily. "That's all they wanted? Count the paper ballots in six counties?" Trump excitedly explored the idea, saw how simple it would be, and even brought up the possibility that it might not be too late, with his last 48 hours in office, to cause it to happen. The meeting dragged on well over an hour, the two sources told me, and they left with Trump fired up about the idea, with instructions given to them that they should figure out by the end of that afternoon a way it could be executed in the last two days he had as President.

An hour later their office got a phone call: the President had had further consultations with senior staff, had been dissuaded, and the staffers were instructed to drop the idea.

Chapter 9: The Aftermath

In my humble tale thus far I sought to stick to what I saw, what I heard, and what I knew. In this final chapter I will cover what I *think*. As I skim across a number of subjects I will thus be less rigorous and more given to speculation than in previous chapters (which I concede here).

PRESIDENT* JOSEPH BIDEN

> *"You must never confuse faith that you will prevail in the end—which you can never afford to lose —with the discipline to confront the most brutal facts of your current reality, whatever they might be."*

- James Stockdale

Our Founding Fathers designed a Constitutional process for selecting our President. I recognize that the Constitutional process ran its course and selected Joe Biden as President. So Biden *is* President.

Federalist Paper 68 (Hamilton) argued that one thing our process had to recommend it was that it would filter out certain types of politicians and select for others (one wonders which describes Biden):

> "Talents for low intrigue, and the little arts of popularity, may alone suffice to elevate a man to the first honors in a single State; but it will require other talents, and a different kind of merit, to establish him in the esteem and confidence of the whole Union, or of so considerable a portion of it as would be necessary to make him a successful candidate for the distinguished office of President of the United States."

The drafters also anticipated state level corruption might disrupt a national election:

> "It was also peculiarly desirable to afford as little opportunity as possible to tumult and disorder... But the precautions which have been so happily concerted in the system under consideration, promise an effectual security against this mischief. The choice of SEVERAL, to form an intermediate body of electors, will be much less apt to convulse the community with any extraordinary or violent movements, than the choice of ONE who was himself to be the final object of the public wishes. And as the electors, chosen in each State, are to assemble and vote in the State in which they are chosen, this detached and divided situation will expose them much less to heats and ferments, which might be communicated from them to the people, than if they were all to be convened at one time, in one place."

By bifurcating the choice into (on the one hand) "an intermediate body of electors", and (on the other hand) a Senate to examine and formally accept the votes of the Electoral College, something else was accomplished. Because elections may degenerate into debate about corruption, at the end of the day for an office such as President there needs to be a mechanism to guarantee that a selection is made. The system created by our Constitution, whereby electors are chosen and sent to an Electoral College to cast their votes, then at a later point the US Senate (by recognizing and counting electoral votes) accepts that decision, accomplishes that. No matter what goes on at the state level, no matter how corrupt the events there, there is a US Senate to look at the facts and by accepting electoral votes, certify the decision. That bifurcation guarantees that disputes about election integrity cannot swamp the overriding constraint that by *some* date, a victor must be established. This Constitutional process decides the presidency.

On January 6-7 that process ran its course, and selected Joe Biden. So, again, Biden *is* our president.

Thomas Sowell has pointed out that the Right normally sees fairness as an attribute of *processes*, while the Left sees it as an attribute of *outcomes*. For example, imagine a fire department sets up a system for testing applicants, and the test measures physical and mental abilities related to the job duties, then spits out a ranking of candidates. In the eyes of someone who sees fairness as an attribute of *process*, if the testing made no reference to race and measured abilities related to the job duties, then whatever that ranking is, it is by definition fair. The *process* was fair so the *outcome* is fair. But in the eyes of the Left, if the outcome has too differential a mix of Whites and Blacks, it is unfair. That is why (says Sowell) the two sides argue and never get anywhere. They can argue about "fairness" until the cows come home, but underneath that one word they are arguing about two different things: one is talking about a *process*, one is talking about an *outcome*.

We are experiencing a rare moment where Left and Right have switched sides philosophically. The Left is saying, "The *process* ran its course, Biden was selected in that Senate process, so he is now the legitimate President." Others are saying, "Yes, but that *outcome* occurred only because of unprecedented election irregularities which created an enormous and complex election fraud, which survived because the shot-clock expired on January 6-7, leading to a perverse outcome that is unfair and does not reflect the will of the people." Both are holding, in a sense, just the opposite view about fairness that they normally do.

If nothing else I seek to be intellectually consistent, and I think that justice and fairness are attributes of *processes*. The process mandated in the Constitution (Article II Section 1) ran its course, the Senate looked at the facts (as much as they wished to, anyway), they voted, and so the outcome they generated *is* the outcome. Thus, Biden is indeed President. End of story.

It would be tempting to use the Left's own playbook against it by continuing to maintain, "Not my President!" (as the Left said for four years under Trump). By doing so one could force them to reveal their hypocrisy (as if further revelation were needed), watching them froth over a phrase *they* used for Trump's entire presidency based on a theory of Russian collusion that Robert Mueller investigated and upon which he came up empty. However, I am nothing if not intellectually consistent, and as tempting as it would be to do that publicly for the next four years, it feels churlish. So with regret, I must acknowledge that while the Constitutionally-mandated process was corrupted from its inception by election fraud, the process ran its course, Joe Biden was the winner, and so he is, indeed, the President.

Having acknowledged that, I turn to the world of sports for semiotics. In 2007 Barry Bonds hit home-run 762, the final home-run of his professional career (surpassing Hank Aaron's record of 755, which had stood since 1974). However, because for much of his professional career Bonds turned out to have been using performance-enhancing steroids (BALCO labs' "the Clear", so named because it was not detectable in urine samples until the day it was), Bonds' achievement is noted with an asterisk (often printed in red: "*").

In the National Baseball Hall of Fame (to which Bonds has still not been elected), Bonds' record-breaking 756th homer is displayed with an asterisk:

Hall: Asterisk will be key to Bonds display (*Daily Star*, July 2008)

10 years later, Sports Illustrated wrote a story on the asterisk:

Lance Armstrong won 6 *Tour de France* bicycle races. Yet it turned out he did so with the assistance of performance enhancing drugs so, as the *New York Times* wrote in 2012, his record will forever be marred:

Armstrong, *Best of His Time, Now With an Asterisk*

f ⊙ 𝕪 ✉ ↗

Lance Armstrong said he would not contest the doping charges because it had taken too much of a toll on his family and his work for his cancer foundation. Felix Ordonez/Reuters

Armstrong, Best of His Time, Now With an Asterisk

I now adopt the same typographical convention for President* Biden. Referring to him as "President* Biden" accomplishes two things: it recognizes that he did, in fact, become President through the Constitutional process; it also recognizes that irregularities (such as have been described in this story) marred that achievement. So Biden is indeed President* in the same way that Barry Bonds owns the home-run record with 762*, and Lance Armstrong did win the *Tour de France* 6* times.

Q, "TRUST THE PLAN", AND "THE STORM"

I hear from otherwise sane-sounding people, and read in social media, assertions that Trump is really still in charge, or the military is in charge, or that there is a plan, that this has all been a 4-dimensional chess gambit, and Trump is going to reemerge as President, of the Republic not the Corporation (or some such)

It is time someone tells all such folks: that is all delusional. Trust me, there is no such plan. Trump's people in the Defense Department have all left. There is no network of secret agents ready to spring a trap and restore Donald Trump to the White House. It is delusional to think otherwise. The brutal fact of current reality is that (as a result of a process riddled with election fraud), we have President* Biden. If enough of it could have been unwound by the middle of December, state legislators would have had something to think about in choosing their electors. But the genius of those who designed this scheme was that after the election, they knew they simply had to rope-a-dope for about 6 weeks, from November 3 to December 18, then people would be taking off for Christmas, and nothing would be done between then and New Year's, and people were not even showing up to work in courthouses until January 4....so the grinding of constitutional gears would do the rest of the work for them.

The Senate selected. Joe Biden became our President*. Yes, that really happened. Do not live in a delusion by believing a trap is going to spring, a storm is on its way, and so forth.

THE REPUBLICAN PARTY

As I indicated in Chapter 6 ("The Christmas Doldrums (December 23 - noon January 6)", through this process I saw enough of Republican Party "elites" to understand who they are. Other than a small number of strong players, it is mostly socialites and dilettantes, fat-cats and grifters (e.g., raising $300 million to expose election fraud, then provide no noticeable help: someone should look into where that $300 million went).

I advise the Reader: Never give a dollar to the Republican Party again.

In these recent months I met people for whom I can completely vouch. Two people of whom I can say, "These two people are fully and entirely about helping the USA, and are not in it one iota for themselves." Those two people are Sidney Powell and Mike Flynn. The Flynn's and a few others have started an excellent organization, The America Project, and they mean business. Give them whatever donations you would otherwise send the Republican Party. They will be putting the money into two different endeavors: one is organized to fight election fraud, the other will be focused on finding the right candidates to back and fund. If you want a one-stop shop, the one place you can give money to help the pro-freedom side, screw about the Republican Party, then remember the people I am suggesting you can trust: AmericaProject.com.

AMERICA'S MAYOR RUDY GIULIANI

I wish to repeat again that I have been a long-term admirer of Rudy Giuliani. I think he is a great American. But at age 76 he was not the right man to manage a complex litigation involving matters cyber, and certainly not while putting a lot of work into a daily podcast and other pastimes. I also believe he is driven by motives like "jealousy over who gets airtime," and not a guy used to working with or seeing females as equals.

In short, he's Grandpa. I love Grandpa. But I don't think the fate of the free world should have been rested on his shoulders. That was an unforced error on the part of President Trump. As much as I kick myself with should-haves and would-haves, at the end of the day I think that, given this one error, no victory was possible. Numerous people who worked with Rudy's senior team independently came to wonder who among its top members were working for the opposition: that is how weak it seemed. There were fine people on Rudy's team lower down, but it was so horrible at the top victory may have been impossible to win through them under any circumstances.

And Rudy should have had better judgment than to take this on.

DONALD J. TRUMP

"The fox knows many things, but the hedgehog knows one big thing."
– Isiah Berlin

The astute reader will notice my ambivalence regarding President Trump. I have included flattering details as well as unflattering ones. I did so because I did not intend this to be a polemic, arguing for one version of the truth. I wrote it from a sense of duty, as I felt I owed it to our country to relate precisely what happened in those days, and what I observed. I have.

What else may I say about Donald Trump? From my hours with him I can tell you he is a smart man, smarter than I expected. He is more soft-spoken and gracious than I had anticipated as well. He is not the monster the Mainstream Media wishes you to believe. He is tuned in on people.

I also think Donald Trump has a taste for chaos (someone pointed this out to me as a trait of those who grew up around alcoholism). One of my mentors taught me that the first task in any leadership situation is to determine, "What's the mission and who is in charge?" One needs clear chains of command to focus an organization. President Trump's leadership style (which is to throw a problem against the wall and have a crowd swarm in to fix it) seems more appropriate to me to running a marketing company than it is to someone running an operation with millions of employees.

Significantly, I think Donald Trump is a 74 year old fellow who has lost friends over the years, and like all men of that age, perhaps clings to his remaining friends too closely. I was inside his operation from the wheels up, and I saw what I saw: Rudy was not capable of managing the effort it would have taken to defeat the Deep Rig. Thinking otherwise was an absurdity. I am not even sure Rudy *wanted* to. Trump clung to Rudy from a place of loyalty, even after Rudy's disastrous hair-dye-meltdown press conference, saying he would not entertain a solution that did not have Rudy at the helm. Donald Trump paid for his loyalty.

Here is another thing to know about President Trump: I look over all the evidence, his refusal to take the 3-foot putt, and it occurs to me that at some level Trump may have *wanted* to leave. Maybe it was his age, maybe it was threats to his family, but it is entirely possible that by the time I met him in December he was looking forward to moving on and golfing (as he slyly hinted to me). He is 74, a tad heavier than he should be, statistically probably has 5-10 years to live, and may well not really have *wanted* to spend most of them doing what he did the last four.

If that is indeed the case... more power to him. He did go to DC and, in one term, leave a mark deeper than most two term presidents. And he did that while having to fight the government itself for every win.

If that is how he really felt, however, it would have been better for him to concede, and not to call millions of people to spend their savings to come defend him. I am not entirely certain he thinks in those terms, however. But it was a confusing time for all.

I have indicated a lot of ambivalence about Donald Trump. But for the first time I have a clear understanding of the meaning of Donald J. Trump in our history. It is not about his mannerisms, his hair, his speaking style, his management style. What Trump did is figure out one big thing:

> *The people of our country are suffering because elites sold them out. The People look at what has happened over the last 30 – 40 years, and know they have been sold out. They understand that when they look at Trump they are not looking at an "elite" but one who wants to stand up (however coarsely) against the elites on their behalf. That is his source of appeal, and that is what causes so many to look the other way on his personal foibles.*

I agree with this worldview. I formed DeepCapture 14 years ago to document a war I would be waging against the same forces. The USA has become an oligarchy, and the oligarchy has two wings: Wall Street and the Deep State. We are a republic grown corrupt, and the nation is not being run for the benefit of the people. Check. Trump's movement is inspired by the same reaction to the world that inspired DeepCapture. Check. Trump gets it.

The problem is that Trump's personal foibles leaked into his management. Even his admirers told me that the chaos I was experiencing was par for the course for four years. Being President is not a branding exercise, and the management style one might take in approaching a branding firm is not right for running an administration. President Trump is intuitive, so it is said, and not one to do heavy homework (e.g. reading a full PDB). In this case, that resulted in him not understanding his full powers or the courses of action that were available to him.

He left the details to personnel, but his personnel choices were terrible.

An important fact to know is that until he was President, Donald Trump had never spent a night in DC. Based on what I observed, my sense is that Trump's goose was cooked the day he fired Mike Flynn (and remember, it was Pence who demanded Flynn leave). For the next four years Trump got managed, got *handled*, by the bureaucracy. It is indeed a wonder Trump got done what he did. But I am confident that had Flynn been there history would have been completely different.

My anguish for Trump is that he wanted to be a great president. The opportunity of the century presented itself, in this form: if he had used his powers under that Executive Order to send in *federales* of one flavor or another to audit paper ballot backups in those six counties, I believe what would have been exposed would have shocked the conscience of America. I believe it would have justified a ripple of such audits around the country, and people would have finally grasped that the most fundamental act of our political life, voting, has become deeply compromised. If the ballots in each of the cities that interrupted their vote counting turned up to be as crooked as I believe, it would have created an impetus for reform around the country, finally. And as that played out it would have changed the political face of America for a generation or more.

President Trump had thrown to him as one of history's greatest hanging curve-balls, ... and he let bat rest on his shoulders. That is why I do not know whether to be angry at him or to weep for him.

"DEBUNKING," RETRACTIONS, CONSPIRACY THEORIES, AND "WHERE'S THE PROOF?"

"Debunking"

A year ago I was in face-to-face conversation with a journalist who asked about Seth Rich. I told her the official story but said it had holes in it, adding that there was an alternative story, which I sketched out. She took out her iPhone, searched for 5 seconds, and said, "Oh no, that's been debunked. That story about Seth Rich's murder has been debunked." What was interesting about it was that she had not actually *read* anything: she had just found a title (the top Google search result for "Seth Rich debunked" is an NPR story: "'Conspiracyland' Debunks Theories About Murder Of DNC Staffer Seth Rich"). That was enough for her.

A friend has complained to me of a husband whose thinking is similarly shallow, and who uses the word "debunked" to forestall having to do any research or thinking for himself. She told me she has a recurring frustration-fantasy of someday bringing another man home to bed and making sure her husband catches her. She dreams he will start screaming at her, "You bitch! You're cheating on me!" Without stopping what she is doing, she told me, she is going to calmly reply, "Oh no Honey, that's been debunked. That theory's been debunked."

So be careful when you hear the word, "debunked". It is a mind-hack that gets people to stop thinking for themselves. Along with the phrase, "conspiracy theory".

Retractions

There are analyses that I have not revealed because they have been muddied up with the subject of retractions. For example, one researcher made an argument from Benford's law (a law concerning the frequency of appearance of leading digits in large sets of data): **"Biden's vote numbers in Michigan do not match Benford's law at a 99.999% significance level" (see** "UPDATE: Benford's Law Has Been Used to Prove Election Fraud in the Past – Joe Biden's Numbers in Michigan are 99% Flawed — TGP, November 8, 2020).

Nassim Talib (whom I respect and admire) challenged this Benford Law analysis on a number of grounds, one being that Benford's Law applies only in data sets with a wide distribution of orders of magnitude. An excellent discussion of Taleb's argument can be found in this video:

NASSIM TALEB WEIGHS IN ON BENFORD'S LAW FOR ELECTION FRAUD DETECTION!!!

Interestingly, that video's conclusion is that Taleb is correct to say Benford's Law does *not* apply here, but that there is much better statistical evidence to make one question Biden's win. That evidence was discussed in an article from The CORTES, "The Statistical Case Against Biden's Win: *Statistics continue to cast real doubt on the probability of a President Trump loss in the election*".

NEWS, ANALYSIS, POLITICS

CORTES: The Statistical Case Against Biden's Win

NOVEMBER 9, 2020 · STEVE CORTES

Statistics continue to cast real doubt on the probability of a President Trump loss in the election.

"The statistical case is, admittedly, circumstantial rather than conclusive...But the numbers also firmly point to the intense improbability of the accuracy of the present Biden lead. The statistical case provides more than enough reasonable suspicion to require hand recounts and immediate investigation into fraudulent activities, including the new damning revelations of on-the-record whistleblowers.... There are four key elements to the numerical thesis...."

As mentioned in this story, Rudy's team generally could not find local counsel in the important states because, once lawyers they started getting death threats (as their Pennsylvania lawyer did), they would drop out. As I have shown, in Michigan an election board member had her children threatened; elsewhere, a state legislator gave vigilante-like instructions to her "soldiers" to take down anyone working to unravel the Rig. We had numerous witnesses around the country tell us they had received threats, and several did receive protection for some time.

Interestingly, though some of these threats were open (e.g., the one *against* the election board member, and the one *by* the state legislator), and even televised, nothing was done about it. It became normalized to make those threats from the Left. I believe it did not take much of that to chill the discourse seriously. Once it was national news that such threats were being made, and that there was no police response, it seemed like the whole nation was disoriented.

That is the context within which one has to take any talk of, "retractions".

The Williams Professor whose affidavit was provided above faced intense professional and community criticism for his work, including within the Williams community. He did *not* retract it but he did agree with the obvious point that his study was only as good as the survey data behind it, which conventional press trumpeted (and exaggerated) where it could:

- Williams prof disavows own finding of mishandled GOP ballots (*The Berkshire Eagle*, November 24, 2020).
- Math Professor Concedes Shortcomings in Analysis of Potentially Mishandled Ballots, Stands by Concerns (*The Epoch Times*, November 25, 2020).

My immediate point is that in an environment where public goon-ism has become normalized, when people have their livelihoods threatened and have no redress, where public officials have their children's lives threatened and the law does nothing about the goon-ism... it may not take too much to get a professor to change his mind. And it is not even clear at all that the professor did.

My greater point is this: I have presented through this work a constellation of evidence, from academics to *pajamahadeen* to videos of events, to findings of various researchers. Some have those have been challenged, a couple those claims of "debunked!" have held, but much more often the debunking has been debunked. The vast majority of what I have presented has not been "debunked" at all, but at best, swept into the Orwellian Memory Hole.

Your decision should be: Has Byrne raised enough doubt in your mind about Election 2020 that you think its flaws should be examined, so that we can guarantee an honest election in 2022?

Conspiracy Theories

One objection I heard along the way to the picture I was putting together was, "It would have taken thousands of people to work this conspiracy!" My answer to that is, "Not at all. In fact, we have a clear picture of how it was done in Georgia: it took a Leninist cadre of six people, who stayed each night in a motel on the outskirts of Atlanta, then spread to their separate regions of Georgia each morning. Beyond those 6, there may have in each state been a dozen or two dozen Ruby Freeman-type of people, sympathizers willing to be given some instructions on how to bend things, but without knowledge of the Big Picture."

In any case, the question of where there was a greater overarching conspiracy has been answered in an odd article that appeared in *Time Magazine*, "The Secret History of the Shadow Campaign That Saved the 2020 Election" (*Time*, February 4, 2021).

"... the participants want the secret history of the 2020 election told, even though it sounds like a paranoid fever dream—a well-funded cabal of powerful people, ranging across industries and ideologies, working together behind the scenes to influence perceptions, change rules and laws, steer media coverage and control the flow of information. They were not rigging the election; they were fortifying it. And they believe the public needs to understand the system's fragility in order to ensure that democracy in America endures."

We dust off the Orwellian decoder rings we put away after the Cold War to decode that paragraph:

- "a well-funded cabal of powerful people, ranging across industries and ideologies, working behind the scenes to influence perceptions, change rules and laws, steer media coverage and control the flow of information" = It's all a psyop.

- "They were not rigging the election; they were fortifying it." = Freedom is Slavery, War is Peace.
- "...Shadow Campaign that Saved the 2020 election". It saved the election from being determine by the People of the United States without the secret manipulations of "a well-funded cabal of powerful people....working together behind the scenes to influence perceptions, change rules and laws, steer media coverage and control the flow of information." I thought the governing principle is supposed to be, "consent of the governed," not "consent of the governed after they have had a well-funded cabal change the election laws and conduct a psyop on them."

In any normal age, the paragraph from *Time* would be recognized as Orwellian Newspeak. It's sort of funny, actually, like saying, "We had to napalm the village in order to save it." A "well-funded cabal of powerful people... working together behind the scenes to influence perceptions, change rules and laws, steer media coverage and control the flow of information..." in an attempt to "ensure that democracy in America endures." Could a worldview sound more Orwellian?

Another of the things most obviously out-of-place is that the side maintaining there was no significant election fraud on November 3-4 has, since then, fought tooth-and-nail against allowing any scrutiny of the systems to take place so that we might know for sure.

For example, in November, a Nevada court gave some cyber-ninjas of my acquaintance an order allowing an "audit" of election machines in that county. When they showed up to look at the machines, the audit was thwarted by election officials who said, "The court order says 'audit' but it does not say '*digital* audit', it does not say '*forensic* audit'," and on that basis gave minimal compliance. They showed some certificates but gave no access to the machines.

Similarly, in Arizona, currently, the Maricopa Board of Elections is refusing to honor a subpoena from the State Senate, a subpoena that a State Court has instructed them to honor: "Maricopa County refuses to comply with Arizona legislative subpoena for election evidence: *Board for state's largest county, encompassing Phoenix, votes 4-1 to go to court to fight turning over ballot data and machines*".

Fulton County, Georgia defied a unanimous legislative mandate demanding a complete forensic audit. Instead, as I indicated, six hours after that mandate was given, Enterprise vans whisked ballots out of the warehouse, and the next day a shredding company in the next county was engaged to shred ballots, paid for by an employee of Dominion Voting with, I am informed, a company credit card. The man directed to perform the forensic audit was shot at ("Pulitzer And His Team Were Given Directive To Identify Fraudulent Ballots In Fulton County – Yesterday He Reported That Someone Shot At His Team", January 4, 2021).

And so on across the country: in the face of the most suspect election in American history, there has to this day been almost 0 real inspection of the systems and ballots, and what inspection has occurred has been exaggerated (e.g., Georgia). That's odd, because one would think that those asserting that there was no fraud would welcome scrutiny to establish that fraud had not dominated the election in key spots.

While these machines were sold to election boards as offering transparency, in practice there has been overwhelming digging-in-of-heels against transparency since November 4, and every scrap of information we have obtained was fought for inch by inch.

That is how they ran out the shot-clock on January 6.

There are those who say coyly, "But how do you *know* that cheating occurred?" My answer is, "I think it brazen enough I take it as an insult to my intelligence to be asked to accept (without investigation) that there is nothing to this fact-pattern. However, to be generous, I will stipulate that what we *know* is that six cities play a special role in US electoral politics because they anchor (and thus can flip) six key swing states; those six cities saw bizarre and unprecedented activity on voting night, up to and including shutting down vote counting (the water pipes knew just which cities in which to break?); in each case a spike of Biden votes were injected where counting had ceased and observers had been cut out. That smells like skunk. There is a reason the machines were sold to us as always having the paper ballots as a fail-safe, and if there were ever a time to use it, now would be that time: let's open up the boxes with all the paper ballot back-ups and recount the whole thing on livestream TV. And while we are at it, we should forensically examine the machines as well." That is what should have happened.

By federal law, all the election materials used in the 2020 election must be preserved for 22 months. There are efforts to keep investigations running, court cases and Senate hearings and such. I believe that one breakthrough anywhere will generate evidence that will embolden State legislatures to get more aggressive demanding their own local independent investigations.

Still, the opposition has achieved its primary objective: it made it impossible to audit any of the materials meaningfully before the Senate made its decision on January 6-7. Now it continues the fight against transparency, knowing that revelations that would come from a full audit would shape Americans' beliefs about the need to reform our election systems. With luck, before it is all destroyed, in at least one of the cities in question there will be a real independent forensic audit. If the results are what I think they will be, then that will let an informed electorate make a decision about how many more cities and locations to look at.

WHY DOES EVERYTHING SEEM SURREAL?
THE *WEAK* HYPOTHESIS

What scared both Flynn, Sidney, and me, what drove us both forward whenever we asked each other, "What are we doing here?", was the possibility our nation is living through a psyop being executed with military precision. It sounds far-fetched but to us both it was an obvious possibility: what America has experienced for the last year has been a psyop like ones we have used to destabilize and impose regime change on other countries.

The stages of a regime-changing psyop (per what's known as the "Bezmenov Model") are:

1. Demoralization of the country;
2. Disorientation;
3. Crisis;
4. Normalization.

It takes little imagination to fit to this paradigm the events of the last year:

1. Demoralization of the country – Covid-19;
2. Disorientation – Antifa & BLM;
3. Crisis–election counting stops in 6 cities in 6 swing states, then a surprise;
4. Normalization – the media gaslights anyone who sees anything odd here.

Regarding Step #1 ("Demoralization– Covid-19): how reasonable is it to suspect that Covid-19 may have been used in a plan to hijack the USA? I am not referring to the origins of Covid-19, or asserting that it was deliberately *released* as part of such a plan. Yet however it started, once in the open, does it seem like there were those who sought to take advantage of it?

Might they have wanted the pandemic to be *worse* than it needed to be? Let us look at some things that are now known to be true, but which caused mini-hysterics when they first arose in the public discourse a year ago (NB I'm a *real* doctor, not a medical doctor).

Hydroxychloroquine

In 1983 a couple dozen other college students and I traveled to Asia to attend a semester in Beijing. We all were givn Hydroxychloroquine to take prophylactically while there, increasing the dose at the onset of malarial symptoms. Hydroxychloroquine had been around for decades back then: I vaguely remember a warning that slight dizziness might occur when one first took it, and a statistic like, "Of people who take it daily for 10 years, 2% develop heart arrhythmia." But other than that HCQ was described to us as quite benign.

After a year in China I lived in the north of Thailand for five months. There I would see in dusty villages on store shelves: one bottle containing aspirin, one bottle containing hydroxychloroquine, both sold by the pill for 5 cents. When one had malarial symptoms, one bought a handful of hydroxychloroquine pills and treated oneself, just as one had a tooth-ache one bought a handful of aspirin and treated oneself. Hydroxychloroquine was sold to kids with no more thought than one would give selling a few pills of aspirin to a 12 year old with a tooth-ache.

Thus, it was with some surprise that, when last Spring doctors started reporting favorable results with early treatment of Covid-19 using hydroxychloroquine, I saw the Mainstream Media go apoplectic about this suddenly-dangerous HCQ. Talking heads on Mainstream Media discussed whether or not *in extremis* they would take hydroxychloroquine as though they were discussing some radical new form of chemotherapy in the event they had cancer. Governors got in on the act, creating special orders making it impossible for doctors to provide HCQ for off-label use to their Covid-19 patients (a rare moment that the government ruptured the doctor-patient privacy within such decisions are normally made).

It reached such a fervor that Jim Acosta (CNN) attacked Trump for including in a White House gathering of Covid-19 survivors, some who had survived by way of HCQ, as though that put them beyond the pale.

In time, hostility to HCQ began abating when it was learned that the study upon which WHO had made its decision had used fake data.

(BUSTED: W.H.O. And Global Governments Used Fake Data From A Suspicious Company, That Employs A Sci-Fi Writer And Adult-Content Model, To Discredit And Stop Hydroxychloroquine Studies , June 2020).

Yet the HCQ hysteria continued to simmer over the course of summer 2020.

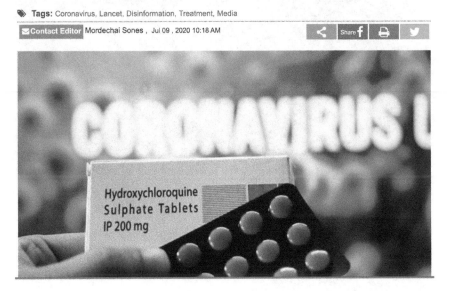

'Media hostility to hydroxychloroquine fuels hysteria about supposed dangers'

According to Duran report media misinformation may be subverting effective treatment to end the coronavirus crisis.

🏷 **Tags:** Coronavirus, Lancet, Disinformation, Treatment, Media

✉Contact Editor | Mordechai Sones , Jul 09 , 2020 10:18 AM   < | Share f | 🖨 | 🐦

- The Israeli newspaper *Arutz Sheva* noted: "Media hostility to hydroxychloroquine fuels hysteria about supposed dangers" (July 9, 2020).
- "Hydroxy is being discounted TOO SOON, say scientists who believe the malaria drug could save thousands of lives by preventing COVID-19 (August 2020).
- "Michigan Hospital Tries To Treat Patients with Hydroxychloroquine; FDA Refuses To Allow It" (Western Journal, August 2020)

By September 2020, antagonism to HCQ had come to seem foolish not just in the alternative press, but to non-obsessed mass media: cf. "The jury is in on Hydroxychloroquine – 'it saves lives': Rowan Dean ".

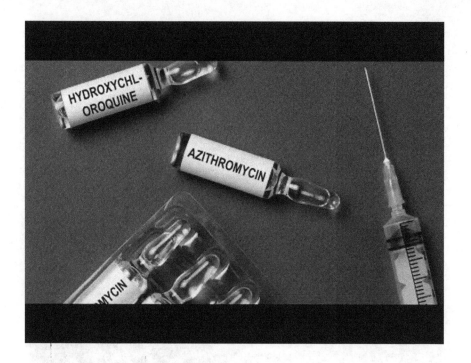

Now the point is no longer in serious dispute: see "HCQ is effective for COVID-19 when used early: real-time meta analysis of 201 studies". Yet in retrospect it is clear that the hysteria over HCQ cost countless lives, and thwarted the ability of doctors to use HCQ to snuff out the pandemic early on.

Ivermectin

Since 1981 Ivermectin has been used around the world as a front-line treatment of parasites (lice, scabies, ringworm etc.) In fact, is is included in the World Heath Organizations List of 40 Essential Medicines (2017). It is benign and ubiquitous.

Yet this benign and standard-issue drug went through the same process of demonization by the Mainstream Media as did HCQ. Eventually, in the face of enough data regarding its efficacy having reached the public, the NIH softened its stance against Ivermectin.

The Association of American Physicians and Surgeons put out a statement welcoming that change: *Association of American Physicians and Surgeons (AAPS) Applauds NIH Revised Stance on Ivermectin for COVID-19:*

"The Association of American Physicians and Surgeons [AAPS] notes that there are now 49 ivermectin studies summarized on c19study.com, 100 percent of which show favorable results" (from the report).

From Australia to South Africa, doctors reported rapid improvements in Covid-19 patients from this cheap and readily available drug. Yet Ivermectin was another drug from which our betters protected us for months of this pandemic, rather than using these safe and dirt-cheap drugs to address early onset of symptoms (which would have done more to "flatten the curve" than all mask press conferences we saw).

Lockdowns

The Left has pushed for the most extreme lock-downs, while President Trump pushed for something more limited.

Sweden, operating from a perspective that was science-based (rather than "hysteria-based" or "politically-based"), instituted a more limited lockdown than anything contemplated in the USA. Their model was to quarantine the vulnerable yet have the rest of society continue their lives with modest social distancing, thus pursuing herd immunity and the least disruption to the economy and civil liberties of the citizens. In other words, the Swedish approach was significantly more Trumpian than Trump (and the precise opposite of the lock-down-mad approach demanded by most of the rest of Europe and the Left in America).

Sweden's strategy turned out to be wisest. Sweden avoided turning into a police state, the second wave they experienced was not larger than the first, and now Covid-19 deaths have tapered to 0 (all data and graphs from World Health Organization website):

Covid-19 Deaths in Sweden

Meanwhile, most of Europe and the industrialized world is experiencing a second wave more intense than the first, and deaths have most certainly not tapered to 0. For example, here are Covid-19 deaths in lock-down-mad Germany, France, and the UK over the last year:

Covid-19 Deaths in Germany

Covid-19 Deaths in France:

Covid-19 Deaths in The United Kingdom

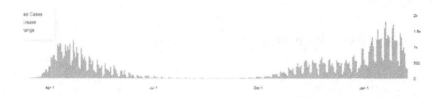

Note the scale dissimilarities on the right: while Sweden has tapered to 0 deaths, Germany, France, and the UK are still experiencing daily deaths in the hundreds and even over 1,000.

THE START OF THE COVID-19 PANDEMIC

Positions thought wacky a year ago that have turned out to be right are not limited to Hydroxychloroquine and Ivermectin. For example, a year ago no "conspiracy theory" was more reviled in the MSM than one that held this pandemic started in a government laboratory in Wuhan.

Yet by the beginning of 2021, we saw articles such as: Corrupt Corporate Media Finally Admits Coronavirus Probably Came From A Communist Chinese Lab (*The Federalist*, January 5, 2021), citing an article in mainstream *New York Magazine*: "The Lab-Leak Hypothesis" (New York Magazine, January 4, 2021).

On February 2, 2021, PBS ran a 90 minute documentary ("China's Covid Secrets"), maintaining that when the Covid-19 pandemic started the CCP engaged in a cover-up.

On February 11, 2021, the Director-General of World Health organization did a U-turn on his previous dismissal of the possibility of Covid-19 originating in a Chinese lab, saying:

> "Some questions have been raised as to whether some hypotheses have been discarded. I want to clarify that all hypotheses remain open and require further study." - *WHO Director-General's opening remarks at the Member States briefing on COVID-19 - 11 February 2021*

One year ago, nothing enraged the mass media more than any espousal of this "conspiracy theory". Now *PBS* and *New York Magazine* (both Establishment) are reporting it as true and WHO has retracted its previous assertion it was untrue.

Which raises a question: *Why at the start of the pandemic were some politicians and media so intent on suppressing possibilities such as HCQ, Ivermectin, and the possible origins of Covid in a Chines government lab and an ensuing CCP cover-up?* It seems they went to extraordinary lengths to delegitimize claims which have since proven true. Does that seem odd?

SUMMARY ON COVID-19

The discourse surrounding this pandemic has been distorted by those seeking to weaponize it politically. As a result, it has inflected more harm on the United States than it had to. The Swedish (science-based) approach would have left us better off, with less harm to our economy and civil liberties, than the path we took. Coupled with the use of two cheap, safe drugs that have been in use for decades, this pandemic might have been snuffed out (or hard-contained) in its infancy.

One group consistently fought such measured discourse, insisting instead on a reaction marked by unscientific hysteria and, arguably, political calculation. For example, among extreme lock-down proponents in the USA have been Chicago's Mayor Lori Lightfoot and New York City's Mayor Bill De Blasio. As soon as Biden's inauguration was confirmed, they switched to less hysterical positions immediately. In Chicago, Mayor Lightfoot immediately reconsidered her former extremism: "Lightfoot Says Restaurants Should Reopen As Quickly As Possible " (*Patch*, January 14, 2021). A similar pattern is unfolding in New York City.

If it is hard to imagine any politician being so cynical as to push for a lock-down that has destroyed tens of millions of lives and hundreds of thousands of businesses (60% of which will not reopen) in order to achieve political advantage.... then you don't understand the Goon-Left.

Above I asked regarding Covid-19:

> "But once in the open, does it seem like there were those who sought to take advantage of it? Might they have wanted the pandemic to be *worse* than it needed to be?

Make your own call.

We now return to the Bezmenov psyop through which we might be living:

1. Demoralization of the country – Covid-19;
2. Disorientation – Antifa & BLM;
3. Crisis–election counting stops in 6 cities in 6 swing states, then a surprise;
4. Normalization – the media gaslights anyone who sees anything odd here.

Regarding Step #2 (Disorientation – Antifa & BLM): One day this fall I was walking in front of the J. Edgar Hoover Building (FBI-HQ) in Washington, DC, when goons came roaring up on motorcycles and ATVs and took over the street, stopping traffic. They did wheelies and donuts for several minutes. Then they roared off. Again, this was on the street in front of putatively the premier law enforcement agency in the world. The guards at the FBI building stood and watched. I understood the message: "This is not the FBI you thought it was, this is not the USA you thought it was."

That, in fact, has been the subtext of the Big Broadcast since June, 2020.

Regarding Step #3 ("Crisis – election counting stops in 6 cities in 6 swing states, then a surprise"): This election is a crisis indeed, but I have already covered this point thoroughly.

Regarding Step #4 ("Normalization – the media gaslights anyone who sees anything odd here"): In September, just four months ago, the possibility of a massive election fraud occurring in the USA was (as I demonstrated in the introduction) a proposition that enjoyed more support across the political spectrum than any single proposition I can imagine. Now the possibility has become inexpressible, even unthinkable, as far as our Mainstream Media is concerned. Even Right-of-Center Newsmax recently saw a host walk off its show, rather than participate in a conversation where the possibility of mass election fraud was discussed.

So why do things seem surreal? Perhaps because you are living through a psyop to take over our country, and reality as you know it is being engineered. Just remember that no, you are *not* crazy, they are just gas-lighting you.

That's the *weak* hypothesis.

WHY DOES EVERYTHING SEEM SURREAL? THE *STRONG* HYPOTHESIS

If the Weak Hypothesis is correct and we are living through a psyop, who is behind the psyop? Strong hypothesis: China is behind the psyop.

I am not a proverbial Old China Hand, but decades ago I was once a Young China Hand. What follows is speculative but worth considering.

Since the Chinese publication in 1998 of: *Unrestricted Warfare: Two Air Force Senior Colonels on Scenarios for War and the Operational Art in an Era of Globalization*, by Qiao Liang (??) and Wang Xiangsui (???), it has been understood that hard-line elements within the Chinese National Security community have been positioning themselves for war with the USA. The "unrestricted" part of "unrestricted warfare" is the part that avoids direct military confrontation, and seeks instead to conquer through non-kinetic means.

In 2015, Michael Pillsbury, a lifelong China-dove (i.e., advocate of helping China modernize and prosper) wrote a book (*The 100 Year Marathon*) where he reversed course. He had been wrong all his life, he said, as he now understood that China had embarked on a 1949-2049 plan to turn the USA into a vassal state. All our work since 1971 and especially since 1990 to help them advance had been accepted by a false friend, who wished to subvert the USA and conquer us.

In this book, Pillsbury discussed a phrase circulating in Chinese national security literature: the "Assassin's Mace". The reference, Pillsbury knew, was to an old Chinese story from the Warring States Period, and refers to a story where one kingdom was due to fight a neighboring kingdom, but one king got an assassin in the opposing king's chambers, and with one stroke, it was over. One kingdom conquered the other without a war. The "Assassin's Mace" means, in effect, a sucker-punch one-punch knockout.

For the last dozen years the Chinese national security literature has had references to an "Assassin's Mace" regard to something planned for the USA. And for a decade our national security community has wondered: "What is this "Assassin's Mace" China has planned? Their new stealth fighter? Ballistic anti-ship missiles? Hyper-sonic missiles?"

I respectfully suggest the reader consider that what we are experiencing is China's, "Assassin's Mace". Nothing would be more of an Assassin's Mace than a scheme to take out the USA with a rigged election that could not be unscrambled through our courts by January 6, thus allowing the Constitutional forces to harden to cement what had been presented as a *fait accompli*.

I am raising this not merely as a theoretical possibility. My colleagues and I discovered ample evidence of Chinese involvement in these election shenanigans. Go through the narrative that proceeds this and note the mentions. Their money shows up in the firms that supply the election equipment in widest use; their components show up in the election machines, and some of our machines are made in China; on Election Day, their IPs show up tickling our election equipment online; receipts from their print shops show up on stacks of ballots in our election operations...

DNI Ratcliffe belatedly delivered his opinion on January 7: he sees more of the intelligence than anyone in government, and his conclusion was that the Chinese had meddled in the election.

If the Strong Hypothesis is correct and this is a Chinese psyop, there is one way you will be able to be able to tell. Authoritarian measures will be imposed within the US (under the guise of stopping something vague like, "extremism"). Biden will fill his administration with China-doves, and he will reverse an Executive Order of Trump's to allow the Chinese to resume building components of our critical infrastructure (e.g., electrical infrastructure). Because the political discourse is constrained by Big Tech and authoritarian measures, within 10 years there will be prison camps built next to hospitals for the purpose of organ-harvesting from dissidents. By that time, Xi Jinping will have a button on his desk: one day he will hit it, the US electrical grid will shut down, over the course of one year 90% of Americans will die off, and the USA will turn into a farm, for which China's 1.6 billion people will be grateful.

Those will be your warning signs if the Strong Hypothesis proves to have been correct.

THE SUPREME COURT OF THE UNITED STATES

We have a Supreme Court. They let us down once, in 1936-1937, when they caved to FDR's threats to pack the Court. The result of their succumbing was that FDR was allowed to punch holes in the Constitution (e.g., Wickard v. Filburn). Through those holes the federal government grew to three times the size it should have been, bankrupting the USA in the process.

So I'd say they owe us one. They owe us one bold save-the-republic move.

The Supreme Court has their chance to make up for that one by riding tall in the saddle now, cleaning up this election fraud and all future election fraud, and thus saving the republic.

They can do it using one principal: stopping voter suppression. Remember, every fake ballot that gets counted nullifies the vote of one actual voter, just as surely as a poll tax (or other forms of voter suppression) would. If the Supreme Court has courage, they will recognize that the moves Democrats made in 2020 to loosen everything that brings integrity to an election, were part of what was, in essence, a massive voter suppression scheme (because industrial-sized election fraud creates massive voter suppression).

This is what voter suppression looked like in Birmingham, Alabama in 1963:

This is what it looks like now:

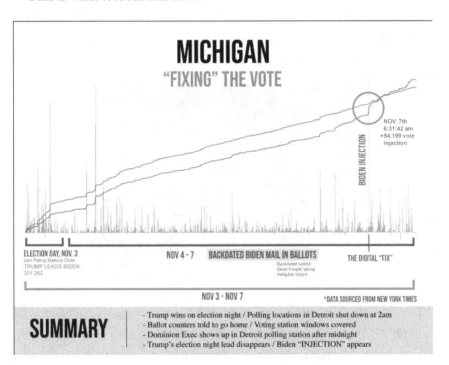

The signs are that in six key states there were collectively *millions* of acts of voter suppression in the 2020 election, by numerous methods. Two generations ago we choose not to live in a world where this occurs:

But in the 2020 election it happened millions of times. Every illegitimate vote in the system is one act of voter suppression against some citizen somewhere who cast an opposing ballot. Thus, in the 2020 election, there were several million of these (without the individuals whose votes were suppressed even knowing it):

I believe the US Supreme Court should, at earliest opportunity, save the republic by recognizing that election fraud is mass voter suppression, and they should create the kind of blanket standards they imposed on states starting in the 1960's. Standards such as: voter rolls must be kept clean; voters have to identify themselves; ballot-harvesting is an invitation to Goon-ism; reconsider using any electronic equipment (Dominion voting equipment is not used in Canada, though the firm is HQed in Toronto); and recognize (with almost all other countries) that mail-in voting is too given to fraud to be used in an election except as a special accommodation.

Take the word of a bipartisan commission led by Jimmy Carter and James Baker:

> "'Absentee ballots remain the largest source of potential voter fraud.' That quote isn't from President Trump, who criticized mail-in voting this week after Wisconsin Democrats tried and failed to change an election at the last minute into an exclusively mail-in affair. It's the conclusion of the bipartisan 2005 report of the Commission on Federal Election Reform, chaired by former President Jimmy Carter and former Secretary of State James Baker III."
> - "Heed Jimmy Carter on the Danger of Mail-In Voting: Absentee ballots remain the largest source of potential voter fraud" (WSJ, April 10, 2020).

The United States Supreme Court is faced with a novel situation. I believe I have presented enough evidence in this work to raise the possibility, in the mind of any sane person, that a well-thought out and crisply executed hijacking of our national election occurred in 2020, by hijacking the anchor city in each of six swing states via election fraud that began with simultaneous and unprecedented shutting down of vote-counting, and continuing through countless forms that have been documented in videos and affidavits and with what forensics have been allowed.

That took a lot of *chutzpah* for someone to pull off. I almost want to tip my hat to it. And I think that if there were ever a time that the Supreme Court should act with *chutpah*, this would be it. All our other institutions have failed us, and this is as serious a moment as the 1960's Civil Rights crisis, perhaps even the Dred Scott decision (another one they flubbed, thus causing Civil War I). If they now give a hall pass to the behavior and activities of Election 2020 that have been extensively documented, it will bring about the end of the republic. Not just from the emboldened current administration, but from the acts of politicians brought to power by future Rigs, great and small, and how that defeats the very concept of *consent of the governed* that is central to our tradition.

The Supreme Court might show some *chutzpah* worthy of the moment, and solve this problem once and for all by recognizing that, thanks to the magic of modern election systems and methods and rules, we are back to is a world where this just happened to millions of people:

So it is not beyond the realm of possibility that the Supreme Court will have a chance to do something as meaningful as they did in the 1960's era, when voter suppression and other matters of egregious civil rights violation came before them.

WHAT SHOULD YOU DO? THREE SUGGESTIONS

We can pull this out if everyone will follow three pieces of advice.
    1) The first rule in all situations (from *Hitchhiker's Guide to the Galaxy*):

2) Remain non-violent. Does anyone not see how much the events of January 6 hurt our cause? There were a *huge* number of Americans on the side of wanting to get to the bottom of election fraud, until the Capitol was stormed. It was a tremendous setback to our pro-freedom side. That may, in fact, be why (to some degree) it was engineered. At this point, the Goon's in power *want* you to go violent, so as to justify them unleashing the FBI and CIA and DHS on you with a vengeance. ***Don't do it.*** Remember the audience: middle America who knows something goofy is going on, but will not side with the team that is bringing violence. So remain non-violent. It is better tactically, and it is better ethically.

- To understand why it is better tactically, please see this es-say:: A Message to Militias Across America Regarding the Goon-Left and Agents Provocateurs (Not the Lingerie)
- To understand why is is better ethically, please see this post: Jerry Garcia on Confrontation & "The Main Asshole"

3. Focus your political attention, ire, and efforts on election integrity. No matter what else you want, you want this first and more.

A philosopher named John Rawls referred to "primary goods" as those goods you want no matter what else you want in life. When it comes to our political life, there is one good you must want beyond all others, and that is election integrity. No matter how strongly you feel about education policy, or abortion, or medical care, or religious freedom, or gun rights, or or or... No matter what your concern is in politics, you need to care about election integrity.

That means: get involved with your local elections board. Run for it if you can. Otherwise, volunteer to work in precincts. Do the 2 days of training. *By November 2022 the pro-freedom among us (libertarians and republicans) have to be election mavens.* We have to be working in the precincts and making sure the Rig cannot be repeated. You have 20 months to prepare: all your political ambition should be focused on this point. There is no point worry about any other political matter, without worrying about "election integrity" first and more.

2022 will be our last shot. If there *is* election integrity, I believe the Goon-Left will lose the House and Senate in a landslide, because Americans already see their true colors. On the other hand, if we do not restore election integrity by then, then next election will also be rigged, and we will have tipped our way into a fascist, authoritarian dystopian version of America, run by Goons.

If that happens, you can be sure that with the backing of China, the tech titans, and America's Goon-Left, then Government of the Goons, by the Goons, and for the Goons shall not perish from this Earth. So no matter what you care about in politics, for the next 20 months turn that care into intense focus on election operations in your county and state (swing states are especially important). These processes are open to the public: volunteer, get inside them, figure out what has to happen to make them run with integrity, and fight for that. That's how we win.

THE FIRST AMENDMENT AND THE COMING(?) POLICE STATE

The beliefs I have espoused here are not in synch with the times. Regarding my ability to espouse and defend such beliefs publicly, the First Amendment seems particularly on-point:

> "Congress shall make no law respecting an establishment of religion, or prohibiting the free exercise thereof; or abridging the freedom of speech, or of the press; or the right of the people peaceably to assemble, and to petition the Government for a redress of grievances."

If our new Congress passes any bill criminalizing people for challenging the integrity of Election 2020, not only would it violate the First Amendment, but it would violate every principle on which this country was founded. So I say to the United States Department of Justice: you are going to need a test case. Choose me. I say that not in a disrespectful James Cagney "Come and get me, Coppas!" kind of way. I mean it respectfully but sincerely. If our government wishes to claim that in America, maintaining and expressing political beliefs such as mine *ist jetzt völlig verboten*, I'd like to know.

So I respectfully invite the DOJ to prosecute me for this four-part statement:

1. I acknowledge that Joe Biden proceeded successfully through the Article II Section 1 Constitutionally-mandated process that selects a president. He thus is, indeed, President. I also believe substantial irregularities affected the election process, and that those irregularities should be studied, discussed, and prosecuted in order to restore election integrity to our nation in time for the 2022 election. Due to these irregularities I write of him as, "President* Biden".

2. In addition, to the degree that Biden tries to loosen rules governing future elections, or changes immigration policy so as to shift voter composition in the USA dramatically, I will claim it confirms my

Weak Hypothesis: industrial-level election fraud rigged the election for President* Biden, the Left knows it, and they seek to change the rules and the electorate now so as to lock in the Rig for future elections.

3. In addition, behind some election irregularities I see the hand of China. Therefore, when President* Biden accommodates China through his appointments and Executive Orders, I take it as confirming my Strong Hypothesis: we are experiencing a Chinese psyop to take over the United States without firing a shot.

4. Lastly, I want those who join me in doubting election 2020 to work ***non-violently*** to pursue our investigations, promote our point of view, and get involved with local election activities across the country, with an eye to restoring election integrity in time for the elections of November, 2022. Every fake vote allowed into the system is an act of voter suppression against one legitimate vote from a citizen somewhere.

If it is or becomes illegal to espouse that worldview... I'll be your huckleberry.

Link Appendix

Chapter 1:

1. Hackers target 30 voting machines at Defcon (CNET News) - http://thedeeprig.com/link/1.1/
2. We watched hackers break into voting machines - http://thedeeprig.com/link/1.2/
3. I Hacked an Election. So Can the Russians - http://thedeeprig.com/link/1.3/
4. Expensive, Glitchy Voting Machines Expose 2020 Hacking Risks - http://thedeeprig.com/link/1.4/
5. Voting Machine Hacks at DefCon - http://thedeeprig.com/link/1.5/
6. Watch this hacker break into a voting machine - http://thedeeprig.com/link/1.6/
7. 'Online and vulnerable': Experts find nearly three dozen U.S. voting systems connected to internet - http://thedeeprig.com/link/1.7/
8. Hack the vote: terrifying film shows how vulnerable US elections are - http://thedeeprig.com/link/1.8/
9. Kill Chain: The Cyber War on America's Elections - http://thedeeprig.com/link/1.9/
10. Researchers Assembled over 100 Voting Machines. Hackers Broke Into Every Single One - http://thedeeprig.com/link/1.10/
11. Princeton Professor Hacks Dominion Voting Machine in Seven Minutes - http://thedeeprig.com/link/1.11/
12. 'Drop and Roll' - How The 2020 Election Was Stolen From Donald Trump - http://thedeeprig.com/link/1.12/

Chapter 2:

1. A PMC Threshold Moment by Billy Starr - http://thedeeprig.com/link/2.1/

2. Americans suspicious and outraged after key Dem-run cities STOP counting votes on Election Day - http://thedeeprig.com/link/2.2/

3. Ballot Counting Is Delayed In These Six States With Legal Battles On The Horizon -http://thedeeprig.com/link/2.3/

4. Burst pipe delays Atlanta absentee vote counting - http://thedeeprig.com/link/2.4/

5. turned out to be fake - http://thedeeprig.com/link/2.5/

6. Evidence Proves 'Burst Water Pipe' In Georgia Was Used As Cover For Secret Vote-Counting - http://thedeeprig.com/link/2.6/

7. Reported Burst Pipe in Atlanta Ballot-Count Area Was Overflowing Urinal: Investigator - http://thedeeprig.com/link/2.7/

8. Suitcases of ballots after hours prove fraud Georgia - http://thedeeprig.com/link/2.8/

9. Georgia State Farm Arena Footage Shows Poll Workers Staying Behind, Pulling Out Suitcases With Ballots - http://thedeeprig.com/link/2.9/

10. Suitcases of Ballots Pulled From Under Table AFTER Poll Watchers Were Told to Leave - http://thedeeprig.com/link/2.10/

11. on gobbledygook reasons - http://thedeeprig.com/link/2.11/

12. Watch: Detroit workers block windows, bar observers from watching absentee ballot counting - http://thedeeprig.com/link/2.12/

13. untoward things were occurring - http://thedeeprig.com/link/2.13/

14. Yes, Democrats Are Trying To Steal The Election In Michigan, Wisconsin, And Pennsylvania - http://thedeeprig.com/link/2.14/

15. WHEN THE VOTE COUNTING STOPPED ON ELECTION NIGHT, THESE WERE THE NUMBERS - http://thedeeprig.com/link/2.15/

16. Dominion Machines Cover Millions of Voters, But Watch How Easy It Is To Rig One of Them - http://thedeeprig.com/link/2.16/

17. Edward Solomon - Geometric Proof for Georgia - http://thedeeprig.com/link/2.17/

18. PA Edward Solomon has found *disturbing* signs of statistically impossible patterns - http://thedeeprig.com/link/2.18/

19. Mass Election Fraud is Popping out of the Walls - http://thedeeprig.com/link/2.19/

20. Dominion Voting Machine Flaws -- 2020 Election Coffee County, Georgia Video 1 - http://thedeeprig.com/link/2.20/

21. Dominion Voting Machine Flaws -- 2020 Election Coffee County, Georgia Video 2 - http://thedeeprig.com/link/2.21/

22. LEAK: Email Allegedly From Maricopa Elections Office Found Issue With Sharpies, Said Use Them On Election Day Anyway - http://thedeeprig.com/link/2.22/

23. MIT statistician shows certainty of massive computer vote fraud in 2020 Presidential election - http://thedeeprig.com/link/2.23/

24. SHIVA LIVE: MIT PhD Analysis of Michigan Votes Reveals Unfortunate Truth of U.S. Voting Systems - http://thedeeprig.com/link/2.24/

25. Doug Wade Interviews Seth Keshel - http://thedeeprig.com/link/2.25/

26. SHIVA Analysis of Michigan Vote Fraud - http://thedeeprig.com/link/2.26/

27. Yale Trained Mathematician Flags 100,000 Pennsylvania Ballots As Likely Fraudulent -http://thedeeprig.com/link/2.27/

28. Ivy League Mathematician Makes A Compelling Case For Trump - http://thedeeprig.com/link/2.28/

29. A Simple Test for the Extent of Vote Fraud with Absentee Ballots in the 2020 Presidential Election: Georgia and Pennsylvania Data - http://thedeeprig.com/link/2.29/

30. Expert: Biden win 'suspicious,' 289,000 election-changing 'excess' votes - http://thedeeprig.com/link/2.30/

Chapter 3:

1. ME-000138-TT - http://thedeeprig.com/link/3.1/
2. http://thedeeprig.com/link/3.2/
3. http://thedeeprig.com/link/3.3/

Chapter 5:

1. MIT Math Ph.D. Dr. Shiva - http://thedeeprig.com/link/5.1/
2. Doug Wade Interviews Seth Keshel - http://thedeeprig.com/link/5.2/
3. Edward Solomon - Geometric Proof for Georgia - http://thedeeprig.com/link/5.3/
4. Smoking Gun: ES&S Transferring Vote Ratios between Precincts in PA. - By: Edward Solomon - http://thedeeprig.com/link/5.4/
5. BOMBSHELL: Antrim County Computer Forensic Report - http://thedeeprig.com/link/5.5/
6. BIZARRE EXPLOSION CRASH IN GEORGIA – KILLS HARRISON DEAL - http://thedeeprig.com/link/5.6/
7. Fiery 3-vehicle crash on Interstate 16 - http://thedeeprig.com/link/5.7/
8. James O'Sullivan, Special Agent at Georgia Bureau of Investigation (GBI) investigating the Harrison Deal car crash / hit was found dead of a "suicide" - http://thedeeprig.com/link/5.8/
9. Ruby Freeman Fraud Videos - http://thedeeprig.com/link/5.9/
10. Ruby Freeman - Screengrab of confession to Voter Fraud Crime - http://thedeeprig.com/link/5.10/
11. CAUGHT: Surveillance footage shows GA poll worker scanning the same batch of ballots MULTIPLE times! - http://thedeeprig.com/link/5.11/
12. Here is Jovan Pulitzer's election fraud investigation report (the U.S. Congress was not interested) - http://thedeeprig.com/link/5.12/
13. MUST-SEE: Jovan Pulitzer EXPOSES MASSIVE FRAUD in Georgia Election - http://thedeeprig.com/link/5.13/
14. When Math in Public is for the Republic - http://thedeeprig.com/link/5.14/
15. Abraham Aiyash doxxed Monica Palmers children, announcing names and school then called her a racist - http://thedeeprig.com/link/5.15/
16. Rep Cynthia Johnson Threatening trump supporters - http://thedeeprig.com/link/5.16/

Chapter 7:

1. Mar-a-Lago was a freak show of D-listers - http://thedeeprig.com/link/7.1/
2. Armed Trafficking of Ballots from election Prep Center to Sheriff Jackson's Office - http://thedeeprig.com/link/7.2/
3. Jerry Garcia on Confrontation & "The Main Asshole" - http://thedeeprig.com/link/7.3/
4. A Message to Militias Across America Regarding the Goon-Left and Agents Provocateurs (Not the Lingerie) - http://thedeeprig.com/link/7.4/

Chapter 8:

1. was shot unnecessarily by police - http://thedeeprig.com/link/8.1/
2. A month after Capitol riot, autopsy results pending in Officer Brian Sicknick death investigation - http://thedeeprig.com/link/8.2/
3. The Times Corrects the Record on Officer Sicknick's Death, Sort Of - http://thedeeprig.com/link/8.3/
4. Capitol Police Officer Brian Sicknick's Mother: 'He Wasn't Hit on the Head' on Jan. 6 - http://thedeeprig.com/link/8.4/
5. 2 Capitol Police officers died by suicide days after the Jan. 6 assault on Congress - http://thedeeprig.com/link/8.5/
6. BLM Antifa Protesters Montage - Mostly Peaceful Protest - http://thedeeprig.com/link/8.6/
7. A Message to Militias Across America Regarding the Goon-Left and Agents Provocateurs (Not the Lingerie) - http://thedeeprig.com/link/8.7/
8. Right-wing provocateurs continue to instigate violence at BLM protests and elsewhere - http://thedeeprig.com/link/8.8/
9. Far-right extremists keep showing up at BLM protests. Are they behind the violence - http://thedeeprig.com/link/8.9/
10. 'right-wing people had done it, in order to provoke violence- http://thedeeprig.com/link/8.10/

11. Pelosi-McConnell refused to increase security! Capitol emergency began before Trump finished speaking - http://thedeeprig.com/link/8.11/

12. Outgoing Capitol Police chief: House, Senate security officials hamstrung efforts to call in National Guard - http://thedeeprig.com/link/8.12/

13. Capitol Police Allow Protesters to Reach the Capitol - http://thedeeprig.com/link/8.13/

14. Cops allow protesters to take Capitol Hill (must see) police department let protesters in - http://thedeeprig.com/link/8.14/

15. DC Capitol Riot Police Stand By While Allowing Mob To Storm U.S. Capitol Building(Jan 6th) - http://thedeeprig.com/link/8.15/

16. ANTIFA CAUGHT CHANGING INTO MAGA GEAR IN BUSHES AT D.C. CAPITOL - http://thedeeprig.com/link/8.16/

17. Patriot Stoping Antifa From Breaking DC Capitol Building Windows - http://thedeeprig.com/link/8.17/

18. ANTIFA given weapons from inside capitol building - http://thedeeprig.com/link/8.18/

19. Capitol police open doors for the protestors. They stand aside and invite them inside - http://thedeeprig.com/link/8.19/

20. Police open the doors of the capital and invite everyone in - http://thedeeprig.com/link/8.20/

21. DC Capital Police Lets Protestors Enter and Storm US Capitol Building - http://thedeeprig.com/link/8.21/

22. DC Capital Police Allowing Protestors To Enter and Storm US Capitol - http://thedeeprig.com/link/8.22/

23. Capitol 2021 Ashli Babbitt sync edit 2 - http://thedeeprig.com/link/8.23/

24. More Proof of BLM/Antifa Capitol Riot Involvement Emerges [UPDATED] - http://thedeeprig.com/link/8.24/

25. Utah Man with a History of Organizing Violent Antifa, BLM Protests, Was Inside the Capitol - http://thedeeprig.com/link/8.25/

26. NOT MAKING HEADLINES: Utah Activist John Sullivan Organized Antifa Protest Near US Capitol Before It Was Stormed —

Chapter 9:

9. The Statistical Case Against Biden's Win - http://thedeeprig.com/link/9.9/

10. Williams prof disavows own finding of mishandled GOP ballots - http://thedeeprig.com/link/9.10/

11. Math Professor Concedes Shortcomings in Analysis of Potentially Mishandled Ballots, Stands by Concerns - http://thedeeprig.com/link/9.11/

12. The Secret History of the Shadow Campaign That Saved the 2020 Election - http://thedeeprig.com/link/9.12/

13. Maricopa County refuses to comply with Arizona legislative subpoena for election evidence - http://thedeeprig.com/link/9.13/

14. Pulitzer And His Team Were Given Directive To Identify Fraudulent Ballots In Fulton County – Yesterday He Reported That Someone Shot At His Team - http://thedeeprig.com/link/9.14/

15. Bezmenov Model - http://thedeeprig.com/link/9.15/

16. BUSTED: W.H.O. And Global Governments Used Fake Data From A Suspicious Company, That Employs A Sci-Fi Writer And Adult-Content Model, To Discredit And Stop Hydroxychloroquine Studies - http://thedeeprig.com/link/9.16/

17. 'Media hostility to hydroxychloroquine fuels hysteria about supposed dangers' - http://thedeeprig.com/link/9.17/

18. Hydroxy is being discounted TOO SOON, say scientists who believe the malaria drug could saves thousands of lives by preventing COVID-19 - http://thedeeprig.com/link/9.18/

19. Michigan Hospital Tries To Treat Patients with Hydroxychloroquine; FDA Refuses To Allow It - http://thedeeprig.com/link/9.19/

20. The jury is in on Hydroxychloroquine – 'it saves lives': Rowan Dean - http://thedeeprig.com/link/9.20/

21. HCQ is effective for COVID-19 when used early: real-time meta analysis of 201 studies - http://thedeeprig.com/link/9.21/

22. World Heath Organizations List of 40 Essential Medicines - http://thedeeprig.com/link/9.22/

23. softened its stance - http://thedeeprig.com/link/9.23/

24. Association of American Physicians and Surgeons (AAPS) Applauds NIH Revised Stance on Ivermectin for COVID-19 - http://thedeeprig.com/link/9.24/

25. The Association of American Physicians and Surgeons [AAPS] notes that there are now 49 ivermectin studies - http://thedeeprig.com/link/9.25/

26. Australia - http://thedeeprig.com/link/9.26/

27. South Africa - http://thedeeprig.com/link/9.27/

28. WHO Coronavirus Disease (COVID-19) Dashboard - http://thedeeprig.com/link/9.28/

29. Corrupt Corporate Media Finally Admits Coronavirus Probably Came From A Communist Chinese Lab - http://thedeeprig.com/link/9.29/

30. The Lab-Leak Hypothesis - http://thedeeprig.com/link/9.30/

31. China's COVID Secrets - http://thedeeprig.com/link/9.31/

32. WHO Director-General's opening remarks at the Member States briefing on COVID-19 - 11 February 2021 - http://thedeeprig.com/link/9.32/

33. Lightfoot Says Restaurants Should Reopen As Quickly As Possible - http://thedeeprig.com/link/9.33/

34. as I demonstrated in the introduction - http://thedeeprig.com/link/9.34/

35. Newsmax anchor walks out of live interview with My Pillow's Mike Lindell | New York Post - http://thedeeprig.com/link/9.35/

36. The Hundred-Year Marathon - http://thedeeprig.com/link/9.36/

37. Dominion voting equipment is not used in Canada, though the firm is HQed in Toronto - http://thedeeprig.com/link/9.37/

38. Heed Jimmy Carter on the Danger of Mail-In Voting - http://thedeeprig.com/link/9.38/

39. A Message to Militias Across America Regarding the Goon-Left and Agents Provocateurs (Not the Lingerie) - http://thedeeprig.com/link/9.39/

ABOUT THE AUTHOR

Patrick Byrne earned a Certificate from Beijing Normal University, a Dartmouth BA, Cambridge M.Phil (as a Marshall Scholar), and a Stanford PhD. Twenty years later, Byrne was named *National Entrepreneur of the Year* by Ernst & Young. That 20 years was one of toil, sweat, David vs. Goliath matches, breakthrough discoveries, losses, and (occasionally) victories. Along the way, in 2004 Byrne and the oligarchy got cross-wise, and they have been at odds ever since. He believes the oligarchy has two wings, Wall Street and the Deep State, and that he has them cornered.